STAYING CANADIAN:
The Struggle Against UDI

Keith Henderson

Belle Lea Acres

R.R.4 Peterborough Ontario K9J 6X5
Canada   Phone(705) 742-9901

LIVRES
DC
BOOKS

Cover design by Gerald Luxton.

Designed and typeset in Book Antiqua
by DCAD Enterprises, Montreal.

Printed and bound in Canada by Marquis.

Dépot légal, Bibliothèque nationale du Québec
and the National Library of Canada, 4th trimester, 1997.

Canadian Cataloguing in Publication Data.

Henderson, Keith, 1945 —
Staying Canadian: the Struggle against UDI

Collection of essays and columns by Keith Henderson and others.
Includes index.
ISBN 0-919688-33-0 (bound) —
ISBN 0-919688-31-4 (pbk.)

1. Quebec (Province) — History — Autonomy and independence
movements. 2. Quebec (Province) — Politics and government —
1994- I. Title.

FC2926.9.S4H45 1997   971.4'04   C97-901121-3
F1053.2.H45   1997

DC Books, 950 rue Decarie, Box 662, Montreal, Que., H4L 4V9

For Stephanie, Andrew, Brent, Giuliana, Dave, Hélène and all the Equality volunteers whose struggle has made the difference…

THE CANADA COUNCIL | LE CONSEIL DES ARTS
FOR THE ARTS | DU CANADA
SINCE 1957 | DEPUIS 1957

Table of Contents

STAYING CANADIAN:
The Struggle Against UDI

In early 1996, after the McGill Moot Court meeting that put partition on the national agenda, Financial Post *editor Diane Francis met with me and Brent Tyler of the* Special Committee for Canadian Unity *for a wide-ranging discussion she would later write about in her book* Fighting for Canada:

> *I flew to Montreal on February 1 to meet Andrew Male, Keith Henderson, and Brent Tyler. For nearly five hours in the Ritz's bar we debated and discussed a range of issues over lunch. As we sat in the corner of the posh bar, several other patrons came over to thank me for my columns and participation in the McGill rally. Significantly, Henderson, Male, and Tyler were ignored, even by people who knew who they were. But they deserved more recognition than anyone because of the amount of time and effort each had dedicated to the cause.*

The Ritz meeting resulted in a Quebec Affairs column in the Financial Post, *the first of which follows.*

Saying 'No in Thunder'

by Keith Henderson:
reprinted from The Financial Post
February 8, 1996

Counting mother, father, sisters, brothers and their children, my immediate family numbers about 30. Of those, I and my daughter are the only ones left in Quebec. The rest are scattered across North America, from Ontario to California, among the 400,000 Anglo-Canadians Pierre Arbour says left the province since the passage of Bill 101 and René Lévesque's first stab at secession, one of the largest internal migrations in Canadian history. That is what drove me to politics.

It is no small tragedy to watch a once vibrant, confident community turn in on itself, lose its nerve, its sense of place and prosperity, as its institutions, high schools, hospitals, newspapers and head offices close down or move on, or to watch its members' rights get suspended, its public visibility effaced and its very sense of citizenship and national identity eroded by the threat of ceaseless referendums. No wonder novelist and film-maker Bill Weintraub made the moving van the chief symbol of his documentary (still banned from the CBC) *The Rise and Fall of English Montreal.*

Until recently, appeasing nationalists was one of the favourite pastimes of the Anglo-Canadian élite, who've long practised, in Trudeau's words, "feeding steak to the tiger in the hopes of converting it to a vegetarian." The other was flight. *"101 ou 401!"* the old nationalist battle cry, roughly translated, meant you either loved Quebec's language laws or hit the road. Hundreds of thousands of Anglos chose the road. Hundreds of thousands more are checking their maps, as Lucien Bouchard hatches his third referendum. A CROP/CBC poll conducted in early '95 suggested 59% of Anglos would leave Quebec if it declared its independence. A further 15% of Francos would also leave, for a total of one million five hundred thousand Canadian refugees in their own country, carrying with them unimaginable economic consequences for a 'Rest of Canada' hardly prepared to accept them. And yet, until recently, the best anti-separation prescription politically correct Canada could offer its loyal citizens in Quebec was this wonderful C.D. Howe Institute gem from Stanley Hartt: "to protect themselves people would need to ensure that they were living in Canada on the date of the declaration of sovereignty, and so they would have to move before the expiry of the one-year period in section 16 of the Draft Bill...." In other words, if you don't like secession, book passage early.

I've always had a grudging admiration for those 19th century New England Americans, the Thoreaus and Emersons, Emily Dickensons and Herman Melvilles, sons and daughters of Puritans for whom principle was not always something you earned interest on. Melville comes to mind, because at the end of that craggy, cantankerous tale *Bartleby the Scrivener,* Bartleby decides that his true motto is "Say No in thunder."

That, it seems to me, is what Canadians were trying to say to the Charlottetown Accord, what they'd like to have said to separatists, what ought to have been said to those who told us we had to move to be a Canadian in our own country, to those like the PQ's intergovernmental affairs minister Jacques Brassard who just the other day equated natives with 'bandits' and threatened to sic the *Sureté du Québec* on anyone who wouldn't obey revolutionary justice in a sovereign Quebec. We should have said "No in thunder" to those in Ottawa who wouldn't challenge illegal laws before the courts, who wouldn't guarantee our right to stay Canadian come what may, and who accused loyal Canadians of being extremists when they asked for the protection of their countrymen against sedition. Good, solid Bartlebys are what we should have had.

Instead what we got was the point-shavers, the cottage industry constitutional crowd, the Mulroney cronies, appeasers and accommodaters all who ran the disastrous YES...BUT campaign that passed for a NO in October '95. So much so that when one businessman got up in the heat of the moment and said we ought to 'crush the separatists,' spineless federalists crawled all over themselves the next day trying to apologize for the man. Daniel 'Canada's-negotiable-but-Quebec's-indivisible' Johnson said we didn't want to crush anybody and repeated that independence is a dream Quebecers have that he'd never want stricken from their hearts. After suppressing anybody that wanted to say NO any louder, Quebec Liberals got the victory they played for — a virtual tie, leaving the knife firmly at the throat of the country, the same knife their fingerprints have been all over for years.

Pierre Elliot Trudeau hated that blackmail and had the courage to say so. Maybe, just maybe, there's another Bartleby in the House.

The Struggle Against UDI
Moral & Intellectual Underpinnings

Stephen Scott is a Professor of Constitutional Law at McGill. He has contributed to numerous academic and legal journals and, as an Equality Party expert witness at the Quebec Liberal Party sponsored Bélanger-Campeau Commission in 1991, was among the first to raise the possibility of the partition of Quebec territory in the event of secession. Sparked by the same Quebec Liberals' secessionist Bill 150, Scott's prescient Issues Relating to Quebec Independence first appeared in 1992, one of the earliest warnings about the dangers of the UDI course both major provincial parties have pursued. Stephen Scott is president of the Special Committee for Canadian Unity, has been active in the demand that the federal government face the UDI issue squarely, and is himself an intervener in the federal government's UDI reference case before the Supreme Court in February, 1998.

Issues Relating to Quebec Independence

by Stephen A. Scott

I. Bill 150

On June 20, 1991, royal assent was given to 'Bill 150,' the *Act respecting the process for determining the political and constitutional future of Quebec,* Chapter 34 of the *Statutes of Quebec, 1991.*

On its face the Act neither does, nor commits the province (or anyone acting in its name) to do anything unlawful whatsoever. As you know, it requires the executive government of the province to hold "a referendum on the sovereignty of Quebec between 8 June and 22 June 1992 or between 12 October and 26 October 1992." Section one goes on to read as follows:

> If the results of the referendum are in favour of sovereignty, they constitute a proposal that Quebec acquire the status of a sovereign State *one year to the day from the holding of the referendum.* [The emphasis is mine.]

This, of course, is artfully ambiguous. Such a "proposal," though it will obviously have major political implications, does not, in itself, actually do anything. Even with a YES vote in the referendum, the Act does not, by itself, declare that independence will follow automatically. Nor does it compel anyone else to declare the independence of Quebec. But in the aftermath of a YES vote, it makes the next step completely uncertain. Negotiations, probably. Confusion and fear, almost inevitably. Of this I shall say more in due course, since we must try to contain the dangerous social and economic consequences of the present crisis.

II. The threat of UDI

B ut there is a further and very different reality, beyond the studied ambiguity of the Act. Sometimes explicitly, often implicitly, the dominant and pervasive daily rhetoric of Quebec nationalist politics and journalism claims the right, and threatens the act, of a unilateral declaration of independence or UDI: that is, the overthrow, within Quebec, by revolutionary act and by force, of the Canadian constitution and of the Parliament and Government of Canada. This claim, and this threat, can even be found asserted in official documents of the Province. Is this a flight of fancy? Am I imagining that the sun will rise in the west? As you are aware, the Act to which I have referred creates two special parliamentary committees, one of them called *The Committee to Examine Matters Relating to the Accession of Quebec to Sovereignty*. Its Secretariat has produced, amongst others, a working document dated November 4th, 1991, entitled *L'Accession à la Souveraineté: La Déclaration de Souveraineté*. Its first and introductory paragraph says, in a matter-of-fact tone (the translation is mine) that the document:

> will take it for granted that the declaration of sovereignty presents an essentially unilateral character, without thereby ruling out the hypothesis of a joint Quebec-Canada declaration.

The document even includes some draft declarations of independence.

Let there be no mistake, then, as to the threat: it goes as far as the revolutionary and forcible overthrow of the Canadian state. Let there be no mistake, either, as to the implications of a unilateral declaration of independence. They go far beyond the bare principle of the establishment of Quebec as an independent sovereign state. At stake also are (1) the potentially explosive issue of the sufficiency of a referendum majority; (2) the absolutely critical issue of the boundaries of an independent Quebec; (3) the division of Canada's public debt and public assets; (4) the freedom of movement of persons and property, including money and valuable securities, into and out of Quebec; and other vital matters too.

A revolutionary Quebec government, if it is allowed to establish itself, could decide all of these things for itself and in whatever way it might wish. This, I suggest, is the worst danger of all, for several reasons. First, Canada as a whole might well say YES to the principle of Quebec independence, but only if it is supported by a convincing referendum majority, and only on acceptable conditions: as to debt, for example; as to movement of persons and property, and, most of all, new, and perhaps drastically reduced, boundaries for Quebec. But Canada's views and interests, like those of Quebec's minorities, become utterly meaningless if Canada tolerates a UDI. Indeed, by submitting to a UDI Canada would actually make Quebec independence a realistic, and feasible, option, and thereby permit and encourage it to take place on Quebec's terms. That, of course, accounts for the apoplectic fury of the French-language press (apart from a very few exceptional journalists) at any suggestion that Canada as a whole has the right, the power, and many hope the will, to confront and thwart a UDI. It is the truth which provokes the rage. So long as we allow ourselves to be intimidated or deterred by these outbursts of anger, they will have every likelihood of continuing.

Second, there is the distinct, and additional, danger arising from the widespread public perceptions which are bound to influence the outcome of a referendum. The more pervasively we allow the belief to spread that Quebec, through UDI, will decide, for itself alone, the terms of its independence, most especially its boundaries, the more attractive these terms will be made to appear to voters in a referendum. This danger, by itself, is reason enough for the people, the Parliament, and the Government of Canada to make it absolutely clear that independence by unilateral act cannot, and will not, be tolerated, under any circumstances — clear, in other words, that independence can be achieved only by constitutional means. You will appreciate that, quite apart from any blandishments dangled before them, there will still be many 'strategic' YES voters in a referendum on sovereignty: people who, not necessarily expecting, or even desiring, independence to come about, think that Quebec will get 'a better deal' in negotiations following a referendum if its outcome is YES. They should be reminded that this is a very risky strategy. Politicians, however well-intentioned, from Danton to Gorbachev have found to their cost that they could neither foresee, nor control the outcome of, social forces which they helped to unleash.

Nor, thirdly, dare we overlook the danger of negotiating constitutional reforms on the basis that Quebec can, by its own act, leave the federation. The premises of a negotiation are usually crucial to its outcome. The Canadian federation must neither deliberate nor negotiate with its hands tied behind its back, nor, as at least one *Québécois* nationalist boasted recently in a prominent national forum, with a knife to its throat; nor, again, under artificial deadlines imposed, under threat of secession, by the Quebec government. We seek balanced measures of reform, not acts of desperation. Balanced measures of reform are, and have always been, possible — measures which can accommodate the legitimate aspirations and interests of all Canadians, including Quebecers — without dismantling the federation under the pretext of saving it.

So even if the threat of UDI is merely strategic, or tactical, which it may be, even if UDI is not now planned, either by those who threaten it, or those who sit by while it is threatened, the threat nevertheless has immediate, and dangerous consequences. Nor, I emphasize, can anyone be assured that the threat will not be carried out, particularly if independence negotiations do not proceed as Quebec wishes. That is why UDI must be confronted now. Nor should UDI be confused with indiscriminate violence, which I hope, and believe, will not occur, even if UDI takes place. Apparent tranquillity can prevail while the state is forcibly overthrown, while the levers of power are taken by revolutionary act. The superficial tranquillity then disguises the hidden violence against the whole country. It is all the more insidious on that account. The more firmly Canada now responds to the threat of UDI, the less risk of disorder later.

III. Responding to the threat of revolution

Self-defence is the law of nature. It is the law of nations. It is the law of Canada. It is the moral and legal right both of the individual and of the state. No one, least of all I myself, has ever suggested 'violence' against Quebec or its people, nor even gratuitous force. Nor have I predicted general or indiscriminate violence in this province. But threats of revolutionary secession, especially from prominent political figures and in government documents, cannot be allowed to go unanswered. They must not go unanswered, not even, indeed, especially not, in the face of a French-language printed press and political élite which (with a few honourable exceptions) responds to contradiction on this issue largely with distortion and diatribe, with hypocrisy and dishonesty.

Do not be misled. The Quebec nationalist élite, and their English-speaking fellow-travellers, do not in the least oppose the use of force. Quite the contrary. They really claim that they, and they alone, are entitled to use force, even unlawful force, and even to the point of overthrowing the existing Canadian Constitution and government. They also, largely, exclude any contradiction from appearing as editorial, opinion, or feature material in the French-language print media, now under their effective control. They revile as 'violent,' 'totalitarian,' 'extreme right-wing,' and 'anti-democratic' those who, like myself, demand no more than that the Constitution and laws be enforced. In so doing, they merely demonstrate the need of repeating, in every appropriate forum, an appeal for legality, and for its preservation by the competent authorities under all circumstances, and by all necessary and lawful means. This I will do without hesitation. The nationalists cannot be allowed to control the terms of the debate. I remind you that I have repeatedly challenged the *Parti Québécois* spokesmen to join me in asking the Minister of Justice of Quebec to refer to the courts the questions of law concerning secession and partition. They have always refused on one pretext or another: Monsieur Jacques Brassard (party whip and constitutional spokesman) on November 26 in the National Assembly Committee; Monsieur Bernard Landry, the party's vice-president, a few days later during a radio debate. Their fear of the law is not surprising. Within our community some interest has developed in bringing the issues before the courts. This presents certain technical difficulties. But if it can be done, I think it would help in stabilizing the province before and, probably, also after any referendum on sovereignty.

IV. What is a UDI?

L et us first examine, from a legal standpoint, what is involved in a unilateral declaration of independence. Such a declaration seeks either to seize, or to replace, the existing apparatus of law-enforcement, and to compel obedience to the laws of the new, revolutionary, government instead of those in the existing Constitution or duly made under its authority. Physical coercion of any kind, including I think credible threats, would constitute 'force.' Actions or threats directed against property would (I think) suffice also. To coerce anyone to do, or to refrain from, anything, by way of compliance with the demands of a revolutionary régime, is in my view to use force in order to overthrow the government. The force, in other words, need not be directed specifically at persons in authority. Once steps are actually taken using "force or violence for the purpose of overthrowing the government of Canada or a province," treason has been completed, punishable under sections 46 and 47 of the *Criminal Code of Canada; Revised Statutes of Canada 1985, chapter C-46.* Needless to say, the declaration of independence itself is, under the Canadian constitution and laws, utterly null and void. No one has the slightest obligation to obey either the declaration itself or the régime and supposed laws which it creates.

Those who actually use "force or violence" to give effect to the declaration have plainly (s. 46(2)(a)) committed treason: they would seem clearly to include for example police or prison officers or other individuals who assist the revolutionary government by enforcing its decrees, and anyone who interferes with those judges and law enforcement officers who are, on the contrary, doing their duty to enforce the Constitution and laws of Canada and the province. All who aid and abet these criminal acts are equally guilty: s. 21(1).

What about those who participate in the making of the declaration of independence? Where force or violence are (as they usually must be) either the likely, or inevitable, or the consciously-willed, consequences of the declaration, *the very act of making it* will, it seems, instantly constitute treason under the conspiracy paragraph (s. 46(2)(c)). At all events, the participants in the declaration will be guilty as parties (s. 22; and see also s. 21(1)) to all subsequent treasonable acts, committed by others, which the participants have, by means of the declaration or otherwise, counselled (or procured, solicited, or incited); and, indeed, probably guilty of an offence (s. 464) if, having counselled, procured, solicited, or incited treason, none is actually committed.

In sum, a unilateral declaration of independence entails the gravest crimes known to our law, the gravest threats to our social order, and the gravest outrages upon the rights of each Canadian citizen individually and of all as a group, *even if there is no general or indiscriminate violence whatsoever.* Canada, as an integral whole, is a sovereign state, every part of which belongs to all of its people, so far as political sovereignty is concerned. Only through the mechanisms provided by the Constitution itself can its territory or its institutions be lawfully altered. Change by any other means is the revolutionary overthrow of the state. These are the two options. There are no others.

V. Independence by Constitutional Means

The Constitution of Canada establishes the Canadian federation and constitutes its provinces, fixes their territorial limits, creates their institutions, defines their powers. "The Constitution of Canada is the supreme law Canada, and any law that is inconsistent with the provisions of the Constitution is, to the extent of the inconsistency, of no force or effect:" I quote section 52(1) of the *Constitution Act, 1982*. And again, reading section 52(3): "Amendments to the Constitution of Canada shall be made only in accordance with the authority contained in the Constitution of Canada." Both those rules are self-evident and, indeed, implicit in other provisions. But it is convenient that they are expressly declared.

For the most part, the methods of constitutional lawmaking are set down in Part V of the 1982 Act, entitled "Procedure for Amending Constitution of Canada." In response to some nonsense in the public press, I am compelled to mention, specifically, also section 52(2) of the 1982 Act, which defines the "Constitution of Canada" to "include" certain things. This definition is thus not exhaustive; but its terms do explicitly encompass amongst other things, the Constitution Acts of 1867 and 1982, and all amendments to them. Sections 3, 5, 6, and 7 of the 1867 Act establish the federation by uniting, into "one Dominion under the Name of Canada," the territory of the pre-Confederation provinces of Canada, Nova Scotia, and New Brunswick; they create the four provinces of Ontario, Quebec, Nova Scotia and New Brunswick; and they fix their original boundaries, thereby incorporating and re-enacting, by reference, the relevant earlier legislative and executive instruments. All of this is, therefore, part of the Constitution, and amendable through, and only through, the processes of constitutional amendment. The federal statutes altering Quebec's boundaries, notably the 1898 and 1912 extensions, alter the 1867 Act, and are, therefore, also within the definition of the "Constitution of Canada" in section 52(2). In sum, the status of Quebec as a Canadian province, and its boundaries, are all part of the Constitution, and, apart from revolution, can only be changed by the prescribed methods. To treat this as doubtful, or to assert the contrary, is crude distortion.

What are these lawful methods? The 'general' amending procedure (section 38 of the 1982 Act) may be employed in all cases where there is not some other procedure exclusively applicable, and, of course, it is also the only available method save where the Constitution gives another alternative. Shortly stated, section 38 requires a proclamation of the Governor-General authorized by resolutions of the Senate and the House of Commons of Canada, or of the Commons alone if the Senate will not agree after 180 days, and also the resolutions of the legislative assemblies of two-thirds of the provinces having, in the aggregate, at least fifty per cent of the population of all the provinces according to the latest general census. It should be added that the legislative assembly of a dissenting province can block the application to that province of a section 38 amendment that derogates from the legislative powers, the proprietary rights, or any other rights or privileges of the legislature or the government of the province. As with the other possibly pertinent amendment processes, either house of the federal Parliament, and any provincial legislative assembly, can, at will, initiate a constitutional amendment simply by passing a resolution to authorize the Governor-General to make a proclamation to enact it. If the National Assembly wishes to propose independence, that is how it can do so.

Most observers consider the "general" amending procedure to be the one which, constitutionally, it would be necessary, and permissible, to employ to establish Quebec as an independent sovereign state. It would, however, be possible to make an arguable case for the unanimous consent procedure (s. 41), which requires the consent of the legislative assemblies of all provinces, or else the 'special arrangements' procedure of s. 43, which requires the consent only of the legislative assemblies of *the affected* provinces. The most essential point, however, is that there can be no such constitutional amendment without the consent of both houses of the federal Parliament, or at least of the House of Commons if, after 180 days, the Senate has refused to pass the amendment and the Commons passes it again.

The 'bottom line' is this. The Canadian people, as a whole, through the House of Commons, have the right and the power to say either YES or NO to Quebec's independence; and, if YES, the right and the power to say YES on any conditions they please. That is the incontestable law of the Canadian constitution, the supreme law of Canada.

VI. "Self-determination" in international law

Has Quebec, as a province, or has its population, or has some part of that population a right, as a matter of positive international law, to secede from the Canadian federation with all or part of its territory?

My answer, No, was given to the previously-mentioned National Assembly Committee on November 26, 1991. My opinion drew an infuriated response from some members, particularly *Parti Québécois* spokesman Jacques Brassard. When, some days ago, Chief Ovide Mercredi of the Assembly of First Nations ventured a similar answer, Monsieur Brassard predictably managed to become infuriated once again, and (I understand) insisted that "all" experts had testified otherwise. I suggest he try a career in melodrama when he tires of politics.

Surely, the issue is not whether French-speaking Canadians are a 'people' with a specific identity. To me, they clearly are, linguistically, culturally, historically. But this neither addresses nor answers the relevant questions.

First, the boundaries of Quebec do not neatly define a single 'people' to whom a right of self-determination can be attributed. French Canada is not identical with Quebec. French Canada includes more than French-speaking Quebec, and, conversely, Quebec is not entirely French, linguistically, culturally, or ethnically. Quebec, in sum, is not one people. There are anglophones, aboriginals, and others, with as much claim to being 'peoples' as have French-speaking *Québécois*. Second, even after one has identified a 'people' to whom one could attribute a right of self-determination, the central issue still remains: Does positive international law confer on a group of persons, simply because it is a 'people,' a right to secede from an existing state? If so, what territory is it entitled to?

The nationalists simply take YES for granted, and assume that they are entitled to the whole of Quebec's territory. When their view is contested, they usually respond, not with proof, but with displays of anger, until everyone (or nearly everyone) falls silent. *Parti Québécois* leader Jacques Parizeau invariably starts by arguing that the francophone *Québécois* majority are a *people;* then shifts his ground to insist that *Quebec as a province* has a right to independence as one indivisible unit. To him, no one but the majority of Quebec's electors has any rights of self-determination at all. Native peoples who have surrendered aboriginal rights of property are said to have surrendered also their claims to sovereignty or self-determination. Natives who have, on the contrary, retained aboriginal rights are however said to possess nothing more than property. International law is brazenly invoked as supporting all of his positions. It is one great tissue of hypocrisy, dishonesty, and deception.

A glance at the legal literature doubtless turns up writers who advance theses, sometimes radical, arguing that groups, defined by language, by history, by geography, by religion, or otherwise, situated within a state, do indeed have a right to secede from, and dismember, that state; though (not surprisingly) these avant-garde thinkers are a lot less able to explain how one is supposed to apportion the territory of the state. But the practice of states has proved to be a great deal more conservative. And it is this practice, particularly as defined in formal international agreements, which is decisive of the actual state of international law.

"Despite its invocation in the interwar years, self-determination was not part of positive international law," writes Patrick Thornberry, an English author, in (1989) *38 International and Comparative Law Quarterly* 861 and following, at p. 869. Since the Second World War, the principle has, however, been acknowledged in major international instruments. Article 1 of the *Charter of the United Nations* enumerates the "Purposes of the United Nations," one of which is "To develop friendly relations amongst nations based on respect for the principle of equal rights and self-determination of peoples." There is another reference to this principle in Article 55, under the heading INTERNATIONAL ECONOMIC AND SOCIAL CO-OPERATION. It is important to mention the *International Convention on Civil and Political Rights,* done at New York on December 19, 1966, in force on March 23, 1976, for which Canada's Instruments of Accession were deposited on May 19, 1976, and which came into force for Canada on August 19, 1976. The first paragraph of Article 1 reads as follows:

> 1. All peoples have the right of self-determination. By virtue of that right they freely determine their political status and freely pursue their economic, social and cultural development.

On the face of the principle, it is hard to conceive of any limits to it. In 1991, Professor Lea Brilmayer of the Faculty of Law of Yale, in an article "Secession and Self-Determination: A Territorial Interpretation," published in the *Yale Journal of International Law* (volume 16, pages 177 and following, at 182), noted:

> The self-determination norm, if taken at face value, seemed to require that states be willing to subdivide

indefinitely into an infinitely larger number of infinitely smaller political entities.

But, as the author acknowledged, the practice of states has not accepted such a meaning.

On December 14, 1960, the United Nations General Assembly passed a resolution, No. 1514(XV), the "Declaration on the Granting of Independence to Colonial Countries and Peoples." I reproduce here the three following paragraphs:

1. The subjection of peoples to alien subjugation, domination and exploitation constitutes a denial of fundamental human rights, is contrary to the Charter of the United Nations and is an impediment to the promotion of world peace and co-operation.

2. All peoples have the right to self-determination; by virtue of that right they freely determine their political status and freely pursue their economic, social and cultural development.

...

6. *Any attempt aimed at the partial or total disruption of the national unity and the territorial integrity of a country is incompatible with the purposes and principles of the Charter of the United Nations.* Yearbook of the United Nations 1960 (United Nations, New York, Ch. V, pp. 44 et seq., at pp. 48-50.) [The emphasis is mine.]

...

Patrick Thornberry, in the review which I have just cited, sums it up as follows:

The logic of the resolution is relatively simple: peoples hold the right of self-determination; a people

is the whole people of a territory; a people exercises
its right through the achievement of independence.
(p. 875.)

In other words, the right of self-determination belongs to the whole of the people of a colonial territory, and, *a fortiori,* to the whole population of a sovereign state, not to part of it. I repeat: Canada as a
whole, and in all its parts, belongs to all of its people, so far as its sovereignty is concerned. For certain limited purposes, defined by the Constitution,
parts, known as provinces, govern themselves sepa-
rately, in the exercise of defined and limited powers. The population of a province has no rights whatever beyond the exercise of these defined and limited powers, flowing from the Constitution. A province, as such, has no right of self-determination of
its own.

A second UN General Assembly Resolution
was passed, without a vote, on October 24, 1970. Its
first article approved an Annex entitled *Declaration
on Principles of International Law concerning Friendly
Relations and Co-operation among States in accordance
with the Charter of the United Nations,* containing the
following relevant provisions:

PREAMBLE

The General Assembly,

...

Convinced that the subjection of peoples to alien subjugation, domination and exploitation constitutes a
major obstacle to the promotion of international
peace and security,

Convinced that the principle of equal rights and self-
determination of peoples constitutes a significant

contribution to contemporary international law, and that its effective application is of paramount importance for the promotion of friendly relations among States, based on respect for the principle of sovereign equality,

Convinced in consequence that any attempt aimed at the partial or total disruption of the national unity and territorial integrity of a State or country or at its political independence is incompatible with the purposes and principles of the Charter,

Considering the provisions of the Charter as a whole and taking into account the role of relevant resolutions adopted by the competent organs of the United Nations relating to the content of the principles,

Considering that the progressive development and codification of the following principles: ...

      (e) The principle of equal rights and self-determination of peoples....

so as to secure their more effective application within the international community, would promote the realization of the purposes of the United Nations...

      1. *Solemnly proclaims* the following principles: ...

The principle of equal rights and self-determination of peoples

By virtue of the principle of equal rights and self-determination of peoples enshrined in the Charter of the United Nations, all peoples have the right freely to determine, without external interference, their political status and to pursue their economic, social and cultural development, and every State has the duty to respect this right in accordance with the provisions of the Charter.

      ...

The territory of a colony or other Non-Self-Govern-ing Territory has, under the Charter, a status sepa-rate and distinct from the territory of the State ad-ministering it; and such separate and distinct status under the Charter shall exist until the people of the colony or Non-Self-Governing Territory have exer-cised their right of self-determination in accordance with the Charter, and particularly its purposes and principles.

Nothing in the foregoing paragraphs shall be construed as authorizing or encouraging any action which would dismember or impair, totally or in part, the territorial in-tegrity or political unity of sovereign and independent States conducting themselves in compliance with the prin-ciple of equal rights and self-determination of peoples as described above and thus possessed of a government rep-resenting the whole people belonging to the territory with-out distinction as to race, creed or colour.

Every State shall refrain from any action aimed at the partial or total disruption of the national unity and terri-torial integrity of any other State or country. ... (Year-book of the United Nations 1970, Vol. 24, pp. 788-792; Resolution No. 2625 (XXV)). [The emphasis is my own.]

In reading these documents you can understand why Professor Brilmayer, in the article cited (pp. 182-3), says:

Although some find this hypocritical, international law currently supports the position that anti-colo-nial movements can invoke the right of self-deter-mination, but not groups seeking to secede from es-tablished states. Once free of colonial rule, the newly established states become entitled to territorial sov-ereignty,

and again (p. 177, n. 5):

The opponents of secession are probably correct as a matter of positive law.

In fact, I urge Monsieur Brassard to read his own Committee's working document *L'Accession à la Souveraineté — Le Processus* (October 8, 1991) §3.1(b). It is far from treating his conclusions as self-evident. Obviously very embarrassed by the terms of the 1970 UN Resolution, it finds refuge in equivocation and double-talk.

What, then, are Canada's obligations? The *International Covenant on Civil and Political Rights* was signed after the 1960 General Assembly resolution, and Canada acceded to it after the 1970 General Assembly resolution. In accepting the 'right of self-determination,' Canada thus agreed to a principle with certain well-known and clearly-defined limits, expressed in those resolutions.

In sum, contemporary positive international law on the subject of 'self-determination' does not go beyond attributing a right of independence to the population, as a whole, of sovereign states, as well as to colonial peoples, that is to say, *peoples who are governed by others*, particularly where there is geographical separation, and perhaps also ethnic or other difference, between the imperial power and the colony. Even so, and in any event, the right of self-determination is to be exercised whilst respecting existing colonial or national borders. African states most of all insisted on this. A colonial right of self-determination can have no relevance to the population of Quebec, which is not governed by others. The population of Quebec not only enjoys all civil and political rights, but has in addition a very wide political autonomy, exceeding in practice even that of American states. So self-determination belongs only to Canada as a whole sovereign state.

Representative government has existed in Quebec since 1791, responsible government since the 1840s. The elected representatives of French Canada were willing parties to the establishment of the Canadian federation, and the French-Canadian people have participated in it in the same way as all other citizens, for well over a century. Any hypothetical right of self-determination which might have existed has been exercised long ago.

International law cannot, the Canadian constitution cannot, indeed, in my view, simple common sense cannot, endow particular groups of citizens in a country, whether or not they be concentrated in specific geographical locations, with a right to dismember the country at will and at any moment. Neither individual states themselves, nor the international community, can function in such a way. Indeed, it would seem that, in the minds of most *Québécois* nationalists, referenda rejecting independence, as in 1980, settle nothing. The *indépendantistes* make it clear that votes must be repeatedly held until the answer is affirmative. This is simply piling hypocrisy on top of absurdity. The recent collapse of tyrannical empires and authoritarian states in eastern Europe is the practical equivalent of the collapse of third-world colonialism, and offers no analogy with Quebec, assertions to the contrary notwithstanding.

And bear this, too, in mind. Even if we were to accept a right of secession for the French-Canadian people of Quebec, we would still be left with the questions of (1) the rights of different groups within Quebec to self-determination; and (2) the partition of Quebec's territory: in sum the questions relating to Quebec's divisibility.

VII. Territorial Integrity

This brings me to the crucial question of territorial integrity and of the double standard. For some people, Canada is divisible, but Quebec is not. I cannot accept reasoning of this sort, not as a matter of constitutional law, not as a matter of international law; not indeed as a matter of simple morality. *Any argument designed to prove that Quebec is indivisible proves equally that Canada is indivisible. And any argument designed to prove that Canada is divisible proves equally that Quebec, too, is divisible.* If there is a *Québécois* people, defined by its ties of language, of culture, of history, there are other peoples defined in the same way: notably the aboriginal peoples and anglophones. If some people have rights of 'self-determination,' that is, secession, others must have them equally and in the same way. It is arbitrary, idle, even absurd to insist that the boundary of Quebec alone defines the sole constituency relevant for purposes of self-determination. There are, indeed, several responses to this notion.

First, international law, as well as Canadian constitutional law, both attribute rights of sovereignty, including self-determination, to the Canadian state *in its entirety*: which means, in the end, to the whole Canadian people, which normally acts through its constitutional-amendment procedures. This, of course, means that the only constituency relevant to self-determination is Canada as a whole, so the Canadian border is the only relevant border for self-determination.

Next, if in truth international law does (contrary to my view) grant rights of self-determination to part of the population of a sovereign state, so justifying secession, this right obviously cannot depend on existing boundaries of any sort: not provincial or municipal boundaries any more than national ones. *If any identifiable group has rights of self-determination, all such groups do.* No identifiable minority could then be denied the right to "determine its own destiny." Moreover, this would be their right regardless of the mere accident of their being, or not being, a majority within one or another pre-established territorial unit or political subdivision of whatever sort, now existing, or which may exist at some future time. And it seems to me that members of the so-called 'majority' who might wish to remain Canadian must also have that right.

Lastly, aside from national or provincial boundaries, there are many others: those of municipalities, school districts, electoral constituencies, judicial districts, and many more besides. The fact that a line is drawn on the ground proves nothing in itself, either legally or morally speaking. By itself, no line whatever can create a right to sovereignty for the population which happens to be a majority within its limits. A territorial unit or political subdivision, of any sort whatsoever, *exists only for the purpose for which it is created:* that is to say, for the sole purpose of the exercise of the specific powers which may be granted to it by the constitution and the laws at any given moment. No more, no less. That is true for a municipality, and it is equally true for a province. The Constitution, and it alone, creates the provinces and grants them their powers. A province has neither existence nor powers beyond, or outside, the

Constitution. The population of a province has the right, but only the right, to govern it within the Constitution, whilst respecting the Constitution, and in the exercise of the powers granted by the Constitution. No more and no less.

The Canadian federation is thus fully entitled, if it is prepared to grant independence to Quebec, to impose what terms and conditions it pleases, more particularly as to territory. The decision to permit, or alternatively to refuse, to dismember the territory of Canada, belongs to the Canadian people as a whole, who might and I think, should, speak directly through a referendum, but who must act through constitutional amendment processes, which now consist of federal and provincial legislative bodies. The people of Canada have the sovereign right to say YES or to say NO, to the dismemberment of Canada, or to say YES, but on conditions which they consider proper.

Conditions imposed upon the grant of independence to Quebec would almost certainly address the territorial extent, and therefore the boundaries, of an independent Quebec. In the south of the province, surrounding the St. Lawrence River, there would be matter of the self-determination of persons, or groups, opposed to secession, who would doubtless include many francophones, as well as people of other linguistic groups, and aboriginal peoples as well. Elsewhere in Quebec, those mainly affected would be the aboriginal peoples.

One central question would be the fate of the territories in the north of Quebec, those attached to Quebec since Confederation in 1867, that is to say, those territories, formerly under absolute federal authority, attached by federal Acts of 1898 and 1912. These represent more or less two-thirds of the land-mass of Quebec, not to mention the situs of resources essential to its economy. Even apart from the wishes of their inhabitants, largely aboriginal through most of their extent, there is the decisive fact that these territories, explored by England, were subject to the sovereignty of the English, and later, the British Crown long before the cession of New France in 1763, even though the French briefly took certain forts. The Treaty of April 11, 1713, signed at Utrecht by ambassadors for the British and French sover-eigns, recognized the sovereignty of Great Britain over these territories, which include notably the Hudson's Bay drainage basin. Article X reads in part as follows:

> **X.** The said most Christian King shall restore to the kingdom and Queen of Great Britain, to be pos-sessed in full right for ever, the bay and straights of Hudson, together with all lands, seas, sea-coasts, rivers, and places situate in the said bay, and straights, and which belong thereunto, no tracts of land or sea being excepted, which are at present possessed by the subjects of France.... [The original treaty is in French. This is taken from a version, reprinted from the copy published by the Queen's special command, and reproduced in Rt. Hon. Charles Jenkinson, *A Collection of All the Trea-ties of Peace, Alliance, and Commerce between Great Britain and Other Powers* (London, 1785), vol. II (1713-1748), p. 5 ff. at p. 34.]

These territories having no historic connection with New France or the French-Canadian people, were attached to Quebec by the federal Parliament to form part of a Canadian province, Quebec, and to be governed, by the institutions of that province, as a province and within its constitutional powers as such. Not for any other purpose.

So long as Quebec remains a Canadian province, the Constitution unquestionably protects its territorial integrity. This flows from sections 43 and 41(e) of the *Constitution Act, 1982*. I fully respect the constitutional provisions which guarantee the territorial integrity both of Quebec and Canada. But should Quebec move along the road to sovereignty, whether by lawful means or by revolutionary act, the question is entirely re-opened. Then it would be Quebec which would be seeking to change the *status quo*. So it would be Quebec which would have to accept the consequences. Canada would, in my view, be insane to allow the 1898 and 1912 territories to be torn away from it. And without these territories, it is doubtful that Quebec's independence is economically viable, certainly at a level acceptable to most of its people. The *Parti Québécois'* apoplexy whenever the subject is raised stems from its understanding (1) that Quebec independence can be thwarted by Canada's withholding these territories from an independent Quebec, and (2) that Canada has the power to withhold them.

I am therefore greatly encouraged to see that, in a recent (Angus Reid-Southam) opinion poll, a majority (46% yes; 39% no; 15% uncertain) of Canadians outside Quebec having an opinion responded YES to the question "Should Quebec [upon independence] have to surrender post-Confederation lands?" (*Gazette*, January 16, 1992). This shows that a good start has been made in educating public opinion, although the poll does not address the partition of the southern parts of the province. Ottawa, of course, has so far desperately avoided touching the subject, probably more for partisan electoral reasons than any other. Fortunately other participants in the debate, especially the aboriginal peoples, have been less coy and less timid. But the question is clearly inseparable from any discussion of independence.

You might then think that partition is an obvious right and likelihood if Quebec becomes independent. I think it obvious. Clearly Monsieur Marcel Côté, consultant and economist at the firm Secor, thinks it obvious too. Judge for yourself from *The Gazette* report of Monday, December 2, 1991 (page A-5), carrying the bold headline: *Sovereignty could cost Quebec north, political adviser says.*

Now, Monsieur Côté is an important former adviser and strategist to both Premier Bourassa and Prime Minister Mulroney. He cannot be dismissed as marginal or eccentric. His comments were made during a taping of William F. Buckley's show *Firing Line* for the U.S. Public Broadcasting System, and in an interview afterwards. Here are a few excerpts from the *Gazette* report:

> Quebec would lose the northern part of its territory if the province separated from Canada, a Montreal business consultant said yesterday.... Marcel Côté ... said an independent Quebec could lose some of the land it regards as its own.... "I would say that probably Quebec will be much smaller at the end of the day," he told Buckley. "If Quebec were to achieve sovereignty, it would have to recognize other people's sovereignty. Why should there be double standards?"
>
> ...

But in an interview after the taping, Côté made it clear he wasn't speaking on behalf of Bourassa or the Liberal party. "They don't want to talk about this."

...

However, Côté said he believed non-native parts of Quebec wouldn't have the right to leave an independent Quebec because they would not constitute nations.

...

Even with his cavalier dismissal of the claims of those who are not natives, this is still, for a francophone *Québécois,* very strong stuff. Did this receive any attention in the French-language press? If it did, it wasn't much. Certainly I didn't hear of any reports. You can understand why the French press and nationalist politicians don't want this sort of thing widely heard amongst francophones, least of all from prominent *Québécois* like Monsieur Côté. It then becomes much more difficult for them to marginalize and demonize Ovide Mercredi and others, like myself, who are not *pure-laine* francophone *Québécois.* You can be sure that Jacques Brassard will not go on television to denounce, and therefore publicize, Monsieur Côté's views.

The French-language press, you should now have concluded, has become largely an instrument of propaganda for nationalist opinion. If you don't believe me, wait until the revised federal reform proposals are issued, and see how 'opinion leaders' in the French press treat them. Perhaps then Mr. Mulroney will at last start seeing the point, and not wait until after a YES vote in a sovereignty referendum to confront *them,* and, more to the point, confront the dangerous premises of their propaganda.

A good place for him to begin would be the repeal or revision of the recent Progressive-Conservative Party resolution (No. 244, passed at its Toronto Conference of August 6-10, 1991) recognizing "the right of Quebec men and women to self-determination." This misleading act was one more wild gamble by the Prime Minister with the future of our country, one more 'roll of the dice' with Canada as the stakes, done moreover for narrow partisan electoral considerations and with the obvious reluctance of many Conservatives. Like all other Canadians, Quebec men and women have the right, *as Canadians,* to self-determination. Canada as a whole belongs to *all* of its people.

Given the vast extent of Quebec's northern territories, and their small population, Quebec, even if it had recourse to revolution, would find itself in no position physically to exert the force needed to take these territories away from Canada without Canada's consent or acquiescence, in other words, to change the *status quo* by its unilateral act. The Quebec north, to me, is Canada's winning card, and it must be made perfectly clear by everyone, including the Government of Canada, that this card will be played. The sooner this is made clear, the sooner constitutional negotiations will cease to be a desperate exercise by the whole country to respond to exaggerated demands and artificial deadlines. But the card is meaningless unless Canada makes it clear that it will use, in self-defence, at least the minimal amount of force needed to hold the Quebec north against any attempt to take it by force. The use of air power, and the control of the transmission of electricity to the south, should (it seems) suffice. For even if force is needed to thwart revolutionary acts, we must try to use no more than is necessary.

VIII. Maintaining Law and Order

Most fundamental of all obligations of the state is that of protecting the citizen against domestic lawbreakers and foreign enemies. Since *Calvin's Case* in 1608 (7 *Coke's Reports* 1a) our law has held that the allegiance due by the subject (citizen) is the correlative of the protection owed by the Sovereign.

The very name 'executive' bespeaks the role of the institutions so named, federal and provincial, to 'execute,' that is, to enforce or carry out the law. Their authority and responsibility to do so, within their respective jurisdictions, is of course plain. On the other hand, the nature and limits of their *duty* in this respect are more obscure. As a matter of principle, the duty of the state to protect the citizen does seem clear. But the executive's disposition of police or armed forces is necessarily subject to wide administrative discretions. The courts do not consider themselves, generally, at any rate, entitled to interfere with the executive's decisions as to when, where, and how, these forces should be used. You cannot, in a court of law, oblige the police force to provide you with a bodyguard, nor compel the army to rescue you in a foreign country. So the duty of protection is sometimes said to be one of 'imperfect' obligation.

What would be the rights of a Canadian citizen in Quebec, in the event of a UDI, if the federal law enforcement authorities simply sat back, and acquiesced in the revolutionary overthrow of the state? (I am, of course, assuming that the secession has not been 'legalized' through the amending process.) While one cannot predict with certainty, I would argue that the courts should not permit the executive simply to abandon its responsibilities. Indeed, the guarantee of "life, liberty and security of the person" in the *Canadian Charter of Rights and Freedoms* could perhaps, through the remedy provision (section 24(1)), create a legal basis for the courts to intervene to compel the executive to protect the citizen.

Force is the original sin of states. Let us not deceive ourselves. *Every* government must, in the last resort, use it to ensure compliance with its laws. Prisons and police are proof enough. The governments of Quebec and Canada use force every day.

Most day-to-day enforcement of federal and provincial laws is a matter for provincial and municipal administration, functioning administratively under provincial legislative power, through police and prison officers. On the other hand there are also federal police forces (the RCMP and others), prison officers in federal penitentiaries, and the (federal) armed forces. Federal law-enforcement agencies (including the armed forces) are, and have the constitutional right to be, everywhere in the country. They are not alien intruders. They have no less legitimacy than provincial law-enforcement officers simply on account of the colour of their uniforms or the calibre of their weapons. All law-enforcement officers (including the officers, and men and women, of the armed forces) share the common duty to enforce the constitution and the laws, though some are normally deployed against domestic lawbreakers and others usually against foreign enemies. Are they to submit to the revolutionary and forcible overthrow of the state? Federal as well as provincial officers?

In the last resort, the responsibility falls upon the Parliament and Government of Canada to defend, and to ensure the execution of, the Constitution and laws of Canada, in the face of war, invasion, or insurrection, or other sufficiently grave threat. This entails the final responsibility to protect the territorial integrity of Canada against *all* who threaten it, foreign invader as well as domestic lawbreaker. The Constitution is clear. When provincial institutions *can* no longer, or *will* no longer, maintain the lawful public order, the Constitution and the law, the responsibility of doing so falls upon federal authority. The 1867 Act "should be construed as providing for such centralised power in an emergency situation" because it "has among its purposes to provide for the State regarded as a whole:" *Fort Frances Pulp and Power Co.* v. *Manitoba Free Press,* [1923] A.C. 691 (Privy Council) at p. 704. "In a sufficiently great emergency such as that arising out of war, there is implied the power to deal adequately with that emergency for the safety of the Dominion as a whole" (p. 705). The 1867 Act moreover confers upon Parliament exclusive legislative authority in relation to "Militia, Military and Naval Service, and Defence" (s. 91.7). And the Queen, that is the federal executive, has command-in-chief of the armed forces (s. 15). In the summer of 1990 the Government of Quebec itself was compelled to resort to the Canadian armed forces at Oka and elsewhere, when disorder reached proportions beyond its means to control. The *Québécois* nationalists have a conveniently short, and selective, memory.

Parliament has provided by law for military aid of the civil power, but only at the request of a provincial attorney-general, in Part XI of the *National Defence Act, Revised Statutes of Canada* 1985, chapter N-5; and for several kinds of emergency measures in the new *Emergencies Act, Revised Statutes of Canada* 1985, chapter E-4.5 (consolidating c. 22 (4th Supp.)). However, unlike the former *War Measures Act*, the *Emergencies Act* (in s. 25(3)) prevents the federal government from declaring a "public order emergency" (Part II) *without the consent of the provincial government*, if the emergency's effects are confined to one province. Moreover, even if a "public order emergency" is in fact declared, the federal government's special statutory powers to deal with it are very limited. On the other hand, it may be that Part IV, "War Emergency," defined to mean "war or other armed conflict, real or imminent, involving Canada or any of its allies that is so serious as to be a national emergency" can be invoked against a rebellion. It (by contrast with Part II) confers very broad powers. The statutory language, our constitutional history, and the inherent imperatives of *all* armed conflict, would suggest that Part IV can be invoked against insurrection. But the federal government should also have at its disposal less blunt means than Part IV. So while the *Emergencies Act* contains new and valuable safeguards against abuse, both Acts seem, in some respects, too restrictive to cope satisfactorily with situations where the provincial governments are obstructive. In my opinion, therefore, they both require some revision by Parliament.

We must hope that there will never be a uni-lateral declaration of independence. We must expect of the courts that, if such a declaration occurs, they will refuse to submit to any attack on the Constitu-tion, and expect of the police, prison guards, and other officials, that they will obey the courts. But would a revolutionary government then try to purge the judges? Replace loyalist law enforcement offic-ers?

We cannot blind ourselves to the possibility that the paths of legality may be abandoned. So we must speak clearly and frankly. The use of force to compel respect for the Constitution, the laws, and the territorial integrity of the state, is neither more or less than legitimate self-defence. The odium of resort to force must lie on those who attack, not upon those who defend them. The *status quo* represents at once the rights of the Canadian people as a whole, and also the right of each individual Canadian who wishes to preserve the integrity of Canada. The Ca-nadian people have every right to insist on preserv-ing their country intact. The most ardent *Québécois* nationalists would instantly become staunch adher-ents of the same principles to defend the territorial integrity of an independent Quebec. Here again, there can be no double standard.

IX. What is to be done?

Economic conditions are poor and deteriorating. Fear and uncertainty seem bound to aggravate the situation. Flight of capital from Quebec appears likely to intensify as a referendum on independence approaches. In the event of a YES vote, this may well degenerate into panic. All of this has a real and damaging impact on the whole country.

Partly responsible is simple and justified fear of independence itself. But fear of sudden independence, at an unpredictable date and on unpredictable terms, independence perhaps by revolutionary and unilateral action, also plays a very large part. After all, any government faced with a financial panic has a great incentive to stop outflows of capital. A revolutionary government can do just as it pleases. We face clear threats of UDI, uncontradicted either by the federal or by the provincial authorities. No one knows how or when independence may come. So individuals and corporations can legitimately fear that they must move before independence is imminent. This has all kinds of serious consequences, direct and indirect. Investment ceases; funds leave Quebec. Faced with transfers of bank accounts, say, or insurance policies, from Quebec to other provinces, financial institutions then confront the gravest pressure to transfer their own lending and other investments out of Quebec, lest they be exposed to risk of having liabilities which must be satisfied outside Quebec, whilst the corresponding assets are under Quebec's control.

Anyone who threatens a unilateral declaration of independence, anyone who even tolerates the threat, excuses it, or closes his eyes to it, is therefore in greater or lesser measure responsible for the intensifying crisis. This includes the Governments of Quebec and Canada, the political élites, provincially and yes, nationally also, and much of the press. The French-language press mostly through what it says;

the English-language press mostly through what it does not say. Only recently, and grudgingly, when compelled to do so, have the 'federalist' élite begun to confront the issues publicly. The threat of UDI, however, is still left unanswered. The élites (even 'federalist') are deliberately encouraging, or protecting from confrontation the belief that it is illegitimate for the Canadian state to defend its existence, even against revolutionary acts, within Quebec. I have already given my view of the implications of such a naive course of action, and its real influence on events.

My first prescription, therefore, is for the Government and Legislature of Quebec to pledge, solemnly and publicly, their *unconditional* respect for, and compliance with, established constitutional processes; and to renounce recourse, *in any circumstances*, to illegal or revolutionary means. The Parliament and Government of Canada must also, and in any event, place on record their solemn promise that they will tolerate no UDI or other unlawful or revolutionary action, under any circumstances. This would go far in restoring and preserving confidence.

My second suggestion is that prompt steps be taken, with the co-operation of the Government of Quebec, to place all the relevant legal issues before the Courts.

My third suggestion is that the Parliament and Government place firmly on record their resolve that, in the event of Quebec being given independence, the province will be partitioned, and, in particular, that the northern territories, added to Quebec in 1898 and 1912, will be taken from it. Parts of the province with federalist populations must also be allowed to remain part of Canada.

Opinion must be mobilized; governments and parliaments pressed to act. Now.

The Struggle Against UDI
Quebec Election 1994

*T*he Equality Party began warning Canadians about the intentions of the PQ to issue a unilateral declaration of independence as early as November 1993. After the '93 federal campaign, the Globe and Mail published "If Quebec Decides to go, What Then?" The questions raised were just as pertinent to the June '97 federal campaign but received no clearer answers than in '93.

If Quebec Decides To Go, What Then?

by Keith Henderson:
reprinted from The Globe & Mail
November, 1993

T he amazing fact about this past election [October '93] is not so much the success of *Bloc Québécois* leader Lucien Bouchard and his separatist option, which polls had predicted for weeks, but rather the utter lack of probing questions to the federalist parties, notably the now-governing Liberals, on how they would deal with a separatist future.

Separatists have never been shy about answering 'what if ' questions. If they lose one referendum, they'll hold another. If they win, don't bother asking again. Quebec will be an independent state. And governing federalists have never been reluctant to respond once separatists have lost. "We told you so," is their usual reply. But if separatists win? Here federalists fall into silence, mumbling, and foot-shuffling. "It won't happen," is the prediction we hear most. But what if it *does* happen? The *Parti Québécois'* Jacques Parizeau has already set the date:

June 24, 1995. Federal Liberals and Jean Chrétien will be on the watch. What will they do?

Here are some of the questions that a probing, public-spirited press ought to have asked would-be federal leaders *before* Canadians gave them a mandate to govern the country in these extraordinary times. Is Canada divisible? If so, how? Is all it takes the election of the *Parti Québécois* — a growing possibility, given the success of the Bloc — and victory in yet another referendum, by no matter how small a margin? Would there be negotiations? If so, what shape would they take? What would be on the table? Debt? Citizenship? Boundaries?

Would loyal Canadians resident in Quebec be expected to give up their citizenship and territorial rights even if they should choose not to become members of a new state? Would these territorial rights belong to all those who wish to stay Canadian, or only to aboriginals, as former constitutional affairs minister Joe Clark implied last year on national television? If Canada is divisible, is Quebec?

A compliant press neglected to ask these questions of our federal leaders, leaving potentially millions of Canadians in Quebec unsure of their rights over the next 18 months. The least that can be done is to pose similar questions to the aspiring leaders of the Quebec Liberal Party. These are the people, remember, whose constitutional strategy was to put the knife to the throat of Canada, and whose official constitutional position remains the Allaire Report — i.e. that Quebec should "repatriate" 22 of 25 powers now exercised by the federal government. These are the people who brought us the Bélanger-Campeau

Commission, legitimizing Quebec independence and giving it as much credence as staying in Canada. The Quebec Liberals are the ones who sat Lucien Bouchard on that commission and allowed Jacques Parizeau to name his favourite financial wizard, Jean Campeau, as its co-chairman. They are the ones who passed Bill 150, telling the people of the province they had the right to self-determination and could choose all by themselves whether the map of Canada would stay the same or be irrevocably changed.

Daniel Johnson, aspiring Quebec Liberal leadership candidate, says he is a Canadian first. I would ask him: What happens if another referendum on Quebec independence goes narrowly in the PQ's favour? Would he vote to stay Canadian regardless? Or would he say, "Quebec has exercised its right to self-determination. We are now in an independent state?"

In March '94, Equality MNA Neil Cameron and I went to Washington where, after Lucien Bouchard's speech to the Center for Strategic and International Studies, we held a press conference entitled "Can Quebec Secede Unilaterally?" There Cameron and I proposed that the American State Department state categorically that it would not recognize a unilateral declaration of independence by the Quebec legislature. This the Americans have consistently avoided doing, though the President of France, Jacques Chirac, went on US TV during the '95 referendum and publicly declared France would. During April 1994, "Setting the Record Straight" *appeared in the monthly Quebec publication* The Dialogue *and a version of* "Sominex for Sleepwalkers" *in* The Financial Post, *the latter reprinted in* Le Devoir *the following month.*

Setting
The Record Straight

by Keith Henderson:
reprinted from **The Dialogue**
April, 1994

I t seems our trip to Washington, setting the record straight after Lucien Bouchard ceremoniously upset it, has had good effect in other parts of Canada. You'll recall that Bouchard was asked by businessman and ex-Townshipper Rick Black if Quebec needed Canada's approval to set up shop as an independent country. No problem, said Bouchard in effect. A separatist referendum win would constitute the birth certificate of the new nation. In any event "the state of Canada did not pre-exist the state of Quebec." So there....

Bouchard conveniently forgot, of course, that the Canadian constitution *created* the province of Quebec, not the other way around. He also forgot the Canadian constitution has no provision for secession, so if there were to be a separate Quebec it would have to come into being with the blessing of Canadians *as a whole* or risk what we always risk when we take the law into our own hands — anarchy, discord, and ruin.

Neil Cameron and I made these arguments in Washington and the good news is that others have begun to take up the fight. Allan Fotheringham was the first in a March 5 *Financial Post* article: "The simple notion that a ... Yes referendum automatically means that Quebec can separate is nonsense. ...Those who would ultimately decide if [Bouchard] is allowed to leave, live in Red Deer and Kamloops and Sudbury." Christopher Young raised a related question in *The Calgary Herald:* "One of the problems with separatism, as the Yugoslavs have found, is the difficulty of deciding fairly who will control what land. If ... Quebec has the right to vote for its own independence, don't minorities occupying recognizable geographic areas have the right to take the other option?" — a theme echoed by Michael Bliss in the March 11 *Toronto Star.* "The Canadian secession drama would be further complicated by the likelihood of minorities within Quebec resisting a separatist majority." Bliss went on to speak of Bouchard and Parizeau's stated intent to declare Quebec independence unilaterally, if need be.

> That is to threaten to take illegal action, the consequences of which could be horrendous.... Those who would claim a right to make their own laws would finally have to take the law into their own hands. This would involve force and violence, the use of the police and military, what Americans recognize as the Fort Sumter scenario (which led to the first shots being fired in a civil war most had thought could be avoided.)

The lead editorial in *The Globe and Mail* on March 29 came closest to the heart of the matter.

> Every citizen of this country is a citizen of the whole of the country, and should not be expected to stand

and watch while a part of it is wrenched away.... Separatists routinely invoke the right of self-determination, as if that settled the matter. But the court of world opinion on whose authority they hope to rely, is as likely to ask: self-determination for whom? What of self-determination of the Cree, of the anglophones, of federalists of every stripe? What of self-determination of the Canadian nation? ...Unless M. Bouchard and his colleagues plan a unilateral declaration of independence — and hence abandon all claim to the protection of the law, international or otherwise — then the vote of 2 million or so Quebeckers in a Quebec-only referendum would not, as he pretends, put an end to the uncertainty over the province's status. It would only be a beginning.

Bouchard and Parizeau *et al* do intend a unilateral declaration of independence, of course, and have said so. It is the recommended way of achieving sovereignty, according to Bourassa and Johnson's own Bélanger-Campeau Commission Report. Consequently Neil Cameron and I will be journeying next to Toronto, to set the record straight there. We'll be sitting down in a press conference with Stephen Scott, McGill professor of Constitutional Law, Kenneth McNaught, former Chairman of the University of Toronto History Department, John Thompson of the McKenzie Institute and others, to tell our fellow Canadians and our silent federal government that we want and expect their help. We want a clarification of the significance of referenda in Canada — a defining, over-arching federal law. We want an unequivocal declaration that our rights as Canadians in Quebec will be protected — *now*. And we want a response to the seditious view, held by both the PQ and Daniel Johnson's *Parti Libéral du Québec,* enshrined in Bill 150, that Quebec can redraw the map of Canada any time it chooses. We are Canadians who happen to live in Quebec. We are tired of feeling abandoned and defenceless. We are tired of the silence, because silence means assent.

Sominex for Sleepwalkers

by Keith Henderson:
reprinted from The Financial Post
April 28, 1994

Whatever else you may say about him, René Lévesque was a democrat. He recognized that a government didn't start the process of breaking up a country without a mandate to do so. He also recognized that complex instruments like elections weren't suited to providing parties with mandates precise enough to justify something as momentous and potentially explosive as separation. Hence the *two* referendum strategy of the Lévesque government in 1980 — one referendum to secure the mandate to begin the process of negotiating 'sovereignty-association' with the federal government, the second to sanctify the results.

Parizeau's PQ proposes something entirely different. The mandate to begin the process of dismantling the country Parizeau and Bouchard expect will be secured in the up-coming Quebec election. What follows is clear: a "solemn declaration of intent to seek sovereignty" put before the Quebec legislature, the promulgation of a Quebec constitution, a period of negotiation with the federal government in an attempt to wrest all power from Ottawa by agreement, schedule to be determined by the PQ, and finally, after a sanctifying referendum victory, the "birth certificate" of the new nation, a unilateral declaration of independence, with or without Canada's approval. [Bouchard is already on record during his Washington trip stating that Canadian approval for Quebec's secession is not required.]

The difference between Lévesque's two referendum strategy and Parizeau's one is essential for Canadians to grasp. Parizeau and Bouchard are treating the 1994 Quebec election in *exactly* the same light as Lévesque did the 1980 referendum. For these two gentlemen, electoral victory means the right to proceed with the dismemberment of the country. That is why easy, doctor-do-nothing platitudes about how Canada has lived through a PQ government before, that the 1994 election is *not* equivalent to a referendum, that we are all to 'cool it', take a valium, and relax is like prescribing sominex to sleepwalkers. The fire gong *is* going. Parizeau's short-track referendum process (he's spoken of seeking the "birth certificate" as little as 3 months from taking power) means Canadians could be facing a unilateral declaration of independence (UDI) from Quebec before the end of the year.

The lulled and the gulled in Canadian political circles usually point to poll results here to justify their silence and indirection in the face of PQ threats. "They may win the election, but they won't win the referendum" is the commonly heard attitude. Stranger things have happened, of course, and we are not *there* yet — *there* where debts are portioned out and boundaries redrawn — but what has emerged along the way to *there* may be at least as debilitating to Canadian life as the prospects of actually arriving. I'm speaking first of the elevation of duplicity in the interests of Canadian unity to the level of a high art. The post-Meech Robert Bourassa let it be known to his nationalist entourage that *he* would lead Quebec to sovereignty. He cultivated Lucien Bouchard, helped set up the BQ, but told his anglo-federalist partners it was all a ruse, a bluff to buy time. His Liberal successor Daniel Johnson, a 'Canadian first' who won't sign his country's constitution, has worked out a deal with his federal cousins where he can play nationalist with impunity, bash Ottawa, scupper key meetings, threaten to take his federal friends to court, all it seems with a wink and a nudge and Jean Chrétien's behind-the-scenes blessing. Now it turns out the latest addition to Johnson's 'pro-Canada' caucus is a former *Bloquist* and his chief of staff, Pierre Anctil, the real author of the Allaire Report. In this climate, how much longer will editorialists in major English Canadian newspapers openly demand that their politicians continue to fudge, waffle, and prevaricate "in the hope that we can once more endure as sometimes a great nation?"

The other perversity of this post-Meech phase of Canadian political life is the ostrich syndrome, most prevalent in anglo-Quebec. Sufferers typically refuse to ask questions or to pursue ideas to their logical conclusions. It has been clear, for example, from 1991 onwards what Parizeau's plans were, yet not one journalist has forced the man to state explicitly whether or not he would declare independence unilaterally if he won his referendum, though the intent is implicit in everything the PQ has written and is manifestly illegal under the Canadian constitution.

No one has asked Parizeau or Bouchard if they would use force (i.e. the police) to compel Quebecers to obey the laws of their revolutionary régime after they declared independence unilaterally. No one has considered the intolerable dilemma in which a referendum victory and UDI would place law-abiding Canadian citizens in Quebec. Would administrators continue remitting taxes to Ottawa *despite* directives from Quebec to cease doing so? What would happen if citizens refused to obey these directives? Which law would take precedence?

No one has asked Daniel Johnson how his party would react to a PQ referendum victory. Would the Liberal party stay loyal to Canada or welcome the bright dawn of Quebec independence? No one has asked Johnson if Bourassa's statement in the Bélanger-Campeau Report to the effect that Quebecers are free to determine their constitutional status *by themselves* means that the Quebec government is free to declare independence unilaterally if it chooses. No one has asked the federal government how it would react to UDI or the use of the police to enforce the laws of a revolutionary régime. How would it deal with what McGill Constitutional lawyer Stephen Scott has said "entails the gravest crimes known to our law, the gravest threats to our social order, and the gravest outrages upon the rights of each Canadian citizen individually and of all as a group, even if there is no general or indiscriminate violence whatsoever"? Would the federal government assert Canadian law on Quebec territory? Or would it allow Quebec sovereignty to prevail?

In his address to the York University Gradua-
tion in 1991, former premier of Saskatchewan Allan
Blakeney said, "Our country may be divided. I hope
and believe this will not happen. But if it is a realistic possibility — and it is — then I suggest that we
do some preliminary thinking about the issues that
will arise." With a referendum-election looming and
the PQ poised to assume a mandate to begin the
process of break-up, the time for 'preliminary thinking' is now. Premier Blakeney went on to speak of
the principle of self-determination, of negotiations,
and of new boundaries. But it might be more appropriate first to speak of the threat of UDI from Quebec. Only when we have dealt with that and laid it
aside can we go on to speak meaningfully, should
worse come to worst, about negotiated settlements,
divisions of debt, and redrawn maps.

In mid-April 1994, Neil Cameron and I travelled to Toronto where, in the company of McGill Constitutional lawyer Stephen Scott and a panel of distinguished historians from U of T that included Robert Bothwell and Kenneth McNaught, we called on Ottawa not to tolerate any UDI from Quebec. Presse Canadienne *distorted our purposes by claiming we were asking for intervention from the Canadian army in the event of secession, a version of events that hit the front pages of some French newspapers in Quebec. The stories in turn sparked an aggressive exchange over the issue between myself and Quebec Affairs columnist for the* Gazette, *Don Macpherson, an exchange which has spilled into recent years.*

Time For Answers

by Don Macpherson:
reprinted from the Gazette
April 23, 1994

F rench Quebec received plenty of warnings from outsiders in the past week that the path to political sovereignty would not be the stroll in the park that most of its advocates suggest. Some of the talk was alarming, and perhaps alarmist as well. The Equality Party, which these days seems to prefer to campaign against Quebec nationalism outside its home province, went to Toronto to raise the spectre of armed conflict if Quebec tries to declare independence from Canada unilaterally — that is, without reaching agreement with the rest of Canada first on the terms of political separation.

Conflict would be inevitable if Quebec declared independence unilaterally, the *Globe and Mail* quoted Kenneth McNaught, former chairman of the history department at the University of Toronto, as saying at a news conference called by Equality. And Equality leader Keith Henderson told the same news conference that Ottawa should use force if necessary if Canadian laws are violated in Quebec after a unilateral declaration of sovereignty, reported *La Presse*

Canadienne. Talk about your apprehended insurrections. To the extent that anybody in Quebec still takes Equality seriously, Quebecers must have been surprised, to say the least, to hear the Eeks talking in Toronto about violence, since nobody is talking about it here, certainly not as a means of achieving sovereignty.

But the Eeks' call to arms raises some questions. What if a majority of Quebecers supports sovereignty? And what if there were no violence here to justify calling in the army? How would that look to Quebecers and, indeed, to the rest of the world? Would the members of a democratically elected pro-sovereignty government be arrested and detained? Would the permanent military occupation of Quebec be necessary to keep Quebec in Canada? Would it be effective? Would it be desirable? Back to the drawing board, Eeks.

A more likely scenario was proposed by Reform Party leader Preston Manning on the occasion of his visit to Montreal. It was also more likely than another proposal by Manning, that the federal government use its power of disallowance last used in 1943, to strike down unspecified provisions of Quebec's language legislation. On the eve of his visit, and again during it, Manning said it would be "naive" of the *Bloc Québécois* and other sovereignists to assume or to suggest to Quebecers that negotiations on the terms of Quebec's political separation from Canada would be quick and easy. Manning points out that while Canada might very well agree to negotiate (and there probably would be business and other interests urging it to do so), it would do so in its own national interests alone. It would try to get the best deal possible for itself. And it would not do Quebec any favours for old times' sake.

In other words, it would act exactly as any country does in negotiations with a foreign country, even a friendly one. For that's what a sovereign Quebec would be to Canada. It seems safe to assume that Manning and his party would make sure that this was the case, if such negotiations should take place during the life of the current Parliament. But even if they weren't around, it seems only common sense to assume that he's right. After all, if the United States would insist on concessions from a sovereign Quebec in return for allowing it to remain in the North American free-trade zone, then Canada could, as well. And if it's likely that the negotiations would be difficult, then it's also all the more likely that they could not be successfully concluded in only the eight or ten months, or possibly even less, that Parti Québécois leader Jacques Parizeau is currently allowing between the election of a PQ government and a referendum on declaring (not negotiating) sovereignty.

Which brings us back again to the subject of a possible unilateral declaration of independence (if not the violence that the Equality Party associates with it). The PQ program doesn't say anything explicit about such a unilateral declaration. But then, it doesn't say anything about an agreement with Canada on the terms of separation being necessary before a declaration of independence, either. So, what about it? Would the PQ declare independence unilaterally? And what are the implications? It seems like the kind of thing that Quebecers shouldn't leave only to outsiders to discuss before the PQ asks them

for a mandate to begin the process leading to sovereignty in the next election.

Outrageous Accusations

by Keith Henderson:
Gazette *Letters*
April 1994

D on Macpherson's generally sneering attitude to the Equality Party is his business (and *The Gazette's.*) He is paid to have opinions and he is welcome to them, but both *The Gazette* and he might consider basing those opinions on facts rather than malice. Macpherson knows full well the purpose of our Toronto visit was to raise the unanswered questions surrounding a Quebec UDI, not, as he puts it, "to raise the spectre of armed conflict," still less to advocate the "permanent military occupation of Quebec to keep Quebec in Canada." These are outrageous accusations.

Had *The Gazette* taken as much time to report on what was actually said in Toronto as it has to distort it editorially, readers would have known that the question of the army was raised by a *Presse Canadienne* reporter, Claire Dansereau, not by the Equality Party, and the question was deliberately returned. "Would Jacques Parizeau and Lucien Bouchard use the police to enforce the (essentially illegal and unconstitutional) decrees of a newly 'sovereign' provincial government? That is the *prior* question to which none of us has had an answer," we said. "Until we get one, we cannot reasonably enter into the subject of force or coercion. If Parizeau and Bouchard *do* use force, i.e. the police — and let them say so if this is their intent — then we would expect the federal government to use whatever means are necessary to protect the rights and safety of law-abiding Canadian citizens." That is what was said. At no time did the Equality Party ever call upon the federal government to send in the troops, there being other means at governments' disposal (as everybody knows) to exert Canadian authority in an emergency, the power of disallowance being one. Never did the idea of a "permanent military occupation" arise.

Most reprehensible of all, perhaps, as Don Macpherson well knows, is that the questions surrounding a possible UDI by a Quebec separatist government were raised *first* by the Equality Party in response to Lucien Bouchard in Washington, where we specifically asked the American government to refuse to recognize a Quebec UDI, an initiative the *Gazette* saw fit not to report on at the time. We raised the questions again in a full press package preceding our Toronto visit which we supplied to Don Macpherson so he would be fully aware of the importance of what we were about to do. Not once has Mr. Macpherson acknowledged the Equality Party's leading role in getting these issues onto the national agenda. Not once has *The Gazette* reported on the Canada-wide attention we've received from raising them, or the impressive list of Canadian academics supporting our views — Michael Bliss, Jack Granatstein, Stephen Scott, Kenneth McNaught to name a few. Not once has the newspaper mentioned the motion EP MNA Neil Cameron has placed on the order paper of the National Assembly, calling on the Assembly, now and in the future, to renounce any unilateral declaration of independence by the province of Quebec. And Don Macpherson wonders why we went to Toronto to campaign against Quebec nationalism? All he has seen fit to do is to ignore our valuable contribution, appropriate our questions without citing his sources, and distort our intent. The least Don Macpherson and *The Gazette* owe the Equality Party is an apology.

Henderson's Accusations Can't Go Unanswered

by Don Macpherson:
reprinted from the Gazette
May 3, 1994

K eith Henderson had no previous experience in active politics when he became leader of the Equality Party only a little more than a year ago. But he's proving to be a fast learner when it comes to picking up some of the little tricks of the trade. One of them is, when you get in trouble over something you said, issue a denial. And if you can't deny saying what got you into trouble, deny saying something else. Blame the media for misquoting you, even if it means you have to misquote the media. After all, most people don't have access to the record and can't check what you really did say in the first place. And generally speaking, the media do a lousy job of defending themselves anyway.

Henderson applied this lesson in a letter published in this newspaper a week ago. He was replying to my column of April 23, which he quoted as saying the Equality Party had recently gone to Toronto "to raise the spectre of armed conflict" (if Quebec tried to declare independence unilaterally) [and] to advocate the "permanent military occupation of Quebec to keep Quebec in Canada." He described these as "outrageous accusations."

Outrageous? We'll see what's outrageous. First, the question of armed conflict. In his letter, Henderson said "the question of the army was raised (at the Toronto news conference in question) by a *Presse Canadienne* reporter, Suzanne Dansereau, not by the Equality Party." Now, even if Henderson were right, there is nothing that requires him or any other politician to answer every question he's asked by reporters. If Dansereau had raised the question, and Henderson had declined to answer it, that would have been it, end of story. "No comment" usually doesn't make the front page.

But Henderson isn't right. Equality Party called the news conference. At that news conference, it gave the reporters material that included several statements referring to the possibility of armed conflict if Quebec tried to declare independence unilaterally; some even predicted it. Most of the statements were made by prominent academics. One of them, in a document whose cover sheet bears the Equality Party logo, address and telephone numbers and the title "Setting the Record Straight," is by Henderson himself.

It says a unilateral declaration of Quebec independence would be unconstitutional and would "risk what we always risk when we take the law into our own hands — anarchy, discord, and ruin." And it quotes a newspaper column by Michael Bliss, professor of history at the University of Toronto, warning that such a declaration could have "horrendous" consequences, including "force and violence, the use of the police and military," and referring to the first shots in the American Civil War. So, tell me, who was it again who raised the question of the army? After reading such statements, if Dansereau hadn't asked Henderson for elaboration, clarification or explanation, she wouldn't have been doing her job. And if Henderson ended up taking heat for that, that's his fault, not hers.

Now, for that other "outrageous accusation" I'm supposed to have made, that the Equality Party advocated "the permanent military occupation of Quebec to keep Quebec in Canada." Wrong again. I made no such accusation. What I did ask was some questions. One of them was whether calling in the army would lead to such an occupation.

You see, sending in the army is the easy part. As we've seen elsewhere in the world, what it does once it's in, especially when a good part of the local population doesn't want it there, and when and how it gets out again, are the hard parts. These are some of the things people should think about before they talk about sending in the army. And maybe the Equality Party and its leader should also think about whether such over-the-top talk about worst-case scenarios attracts attention to them but distracts away from the issues they want to raise.

A regular reader of this column (hi, Mom) knows I don't usually respond like this to criticism. If I can dish it out, I should be able to take it. But I expect my critics to be able to criticize me for what I actually write. It's not as though I don't provide them with enough material.

In May 1994, we issued a communiqué calling on separatist leaders to clarify their intentions vis-à-vis a UDI. In June Equality called a press conference in Ottawa to demand the protection of our federal government against the unconstitutional acts planned by the PQ. Jacques Brassard, later péquiste Minister of Intergovernmental Affairs, had stated in Le Devoir in June that a PQ government would use the police to give force and effect to a unilateral declaration of independence. Bouchard's response to the questions we raised was the following: "The Equality Party doesn't know the tradition of democracy in Canada. That's what will prevail and not provocations or references like those made today." Deputy Prime Minister Sheila Copps dismissed our questions by saying there would "never be a positive vote for separation."

How Would Bouchard Give Force and Effect To a UDI?

Press Communiqué:
May 20, 1994

Equality Party leader, Keith Henderson, today asked Lucien Bouchard, the Leader of the Official Opposition in Ottawa, precisely how, following a referendum victory, he and Jacques Parizeau would give force and effect to the Unilateral Declaration of Independence M. Bouchard has just proposed for Quebec.

"Mr. Bouchard said yesterday in France that if Ottawa 'deliberately dragged things out' Quebec would take the initiative and declare its independence unilaterally 'on the date foreseen in the referendum question.' The American State Department has a protocol for recognizing states that declare their independence unilaterally," Mr. Henderson said. "One of the criteria is for a self-declared 'state' to demonstrate effective control over its territory, in Quebec's case the ability to exclude the application of Canadian law in the province. If Bouchard and Parizeau are to be taken seriously and if M. Parizeau seeks election on the platform of a Unilateral Declaration of Independence for Quebec (if necessary), they must tell Quebecers and Canadians how they intend to achieve American recognition of their new state. Would they use force to compel Quebecers to disobey Canadian law? Would they bring loyal Canadians of whatever ethnic origin, aboriginal or otherwise, into line by using the courts or the police? Would they call on separatist units of the Canadian army (if any exist) to defend their illegal, unconstitutional, and revolutionary acts?"

"Since Bouchard and Parizeau are threatening to take the law into their own hands and assume powers they cannot legitimately hold, the time for answers is now — before an election — not afterwards when the dynamics of separation and the potential anarchy, discord, and ruin they entail have set in. 'How do you intend to give force and effect to your unilateral declaration of independence?' Without answers to this question, Bouchard and Parizeau's public musings represent the height of folly and irresponsibility. Nor must Canadians forget that all political authorities in the country, from the prime minister to the provincial premiers, including Daniel Johnson, owe it to Canadians to state *now* how they would respond to separatist attacks on the fundamental law of our land — the Canadian Constitution."

*O*n *June 17 1994, in an open letter to then Quebec premier Daniel Johnson, now leader of the opposition, Equality posed 8 questions we felt unconditional Canadians needed answers to before an election. Despite the gravity of the situation about to unfold, the letter received absolutely no attention in the Canadian press. Needless to say, neither did Daniel Johnson's evasive and vacuous response.*

Open Letter
To Daniel Johnson

June 17, 1994

Dear Mr. Johnson:

C oncern is increasing across the country about the program and intentions of the *Parti Québécois,* particularly their stated desire to secede from Canada, if necessary unilaterally, and to give force and effect to a declaration of independence by the National Assembly through the use of the police and the courts. The course of action threatened by the Official Opposition in Quebec is, I hope you would agree, illegal and unconstitutional according to both domestic and international law. As the custodian in Quebec of Canada's constitution, you are charged, along with the prime minister and the other provincial premiers, with the amendment of the constitution, with the implementation of its provisions, and with its defence, and so I turn to you, in these times of stress and possible future rancour, to pose eight fundamental questions, the answers to which, I am sure, will be of interest to all Canadians.

1. If, as reports have indicated, you are worried about the organized provocation of Canada following a separatist election victory, why have you and your government not formally agreed to the Constitution of Canada and pursued your desire for change through the amending formula?

2. If, as reports have indicated, you believe Quebec cannot afford another referendum, would you be prepared to rescind Bill 150 passed by your government, the enabling legislation for a referendum on Quebec independence between June and October of 1992 which states that "Quebecers are free to assume their own destiny [and] to determine their political status"?

3. If, as reports have indicated, you believe the upcoming Quebec election will have the character of a referendum equivalent to that held in Quebec in 1980, would you explain whether or not you believe a victory by the *Parti Québécois* would constitute a mandate to begin the process of breaking up Canada?

4. If so, would you explain how you and your party would interpret a separatist victory in the promised referendum on Quebec independence?

5. Would you explain if you and your government believe that Quebec has the right to secede from Confederation?

6. If you and your government believe that Quebec has the right to secede from Confederation, would you explain on what basis? [a 50% + 1 majority in a referendum? A Unilateral Declaration of Independence by the National Assembly? A constitutional agreement with the rest of Canada?]

7. If you and your government believe that Quebec has the right to secede from Confederation, would you explain what principles would govern:

    a) the demarcation of the boundaries of the new state of Quebec
    b) the division of federal assets and debts
    c) the negotiations concerning the desire of large groups within Quebec to remain politically and territorially part of Canada?

8. If, as reports have indicated, you believe a *Parti Québécois* election victory would plunge Quebec into "instability and rancour for months," would you pledge to fight to assure that all ridings that vote for your party in the next election will never leave Canada? Would you pledge to fight to assure that all parts of Quebec that vote against a separatist referendum will remain in Canada?

You have stated that the coming months are a time of important choice for all residents of Quebec. I hope you will agree that your timely response to these eight questions will help clarify the meaning of that choice.

Reply from Daniel Johnson

August 17, 1994

I have received your letter of last June 17, in which you acquaint me with your preoccupations concerning the political and constitutional future of Quebec.

The numerous points you raise seem to take for granted the coming to power of the *Parti Québécois* during the course of the upcoming general elections. I don't at all share your pessimism on this question. On the contrary, I think what is at stake in this campaign will be all the clearer once the population has understood the programs presented to it by each of the political parties. I am confident Quebecers will prefer stability to the unknown.

Convinced as I am of a Quebec Liberal Party victory, it seems to me useless and entirely inappropriate to construct all kinds of hypothetical scenarios.

*D*aniel Johnson called the provincial election for September 14, 1994. In late July we had decided to highlight the dangers of a separatist victory, already predicted by the polls. The following, in brochure form, summarized the main planks of Equality's electoral campaign.

Equality Means...
Staying Canadian

50% + 1...
No way to break up a country

The Liberals and the PQ say a 50% + 1 victory in a separatist referendum is enough to break up Canada. The Equality Party is the *only* provincial party that says you can change a government with 50% +1 but not a nation.

Our future...
A Canadian decision

Bouchard and Parizeau say the map of Canada is for Quebecers alone to decide...and Quebec Liberals agree! The Equality Party is the only provincial party that insists Quebec is a province, not a state, and cannot secede without the consent of the Canadian people.

The tools of secession...
A Liberal Invention

Most people are surprised to learn that the legal tools for a referendum on Quebec independence were forged not by the PQ, but by the Quebec Liberals. Liberals passed Bill 150 calling for a referendum on Quebec independence and stating that Quebec was free to determine its political status all by itself. What will Daniel Johnson say if the PQ uses the tools he helped create?

The threat
That never ends...

Bouchard and Parizeau say that if they don't win their referendum this time, they'll be back for another...*and another!* Asked why he didn't conduct his own referendum and end the uncertainty forever, Daniel Johnson replied, "I didn't want the threat of separation to disappear." The PQ and the Liberals are forcing Quebecers to play an unending game of Russian roulette. Our economy can't survive more of this.

If Canada is divisible
Then so is Quebec...

Bouchard and Parizeau say that Quebec can secede with its borders intact... and the Quebec Liberals agree. The borders of Quebec are "inviolable," Daniel Johnson said recently, even though the federal government has promised

Quebec natives they could choose to remain in Canada. The Equality Party is the only provincial party that says, if ever separatists win their referendum, all strongly federalist areas of Quebec should have the right to 'Stay Canadian.' The Equality Party agrees with former Prime Minister Pierre Trudeau's statement: "If Canada is divisible, then Quebec is also divisible."

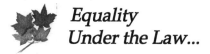

Equality Under the Law...

The PQ says the equality of individuals in Canada prevents Quebec from achieving its 'distinct society'...and the Liberals agree. The Equality Party is the only provincial party that says all Canadians must be treated equally under the law, with rights and responsibilities based solely on their *being Canadian* and not from belonging to any ethnic, racial, linguistic, gender, religious or any other identifiable sub-group.

*O*ur attempt in 1994 to raise the issue of unilateral secession and the right for loyal Canadian citizens to remain territorially part of Canada, come what may, failed. Daniel Johnson's Liberals successfully evaded the issues by telling federalists that if they voted Liberal there would be no referendum and by branding any attempt to explain what they'd do if they lost as 'defeatist.' Throughout the pre-electoral period Liberals had received the unequivocal assistance of the anglo media in Quebec, who steadfastly refused to raise these issues themselves and deliberately blacked out Equality's point of view. The culmination of this media policy of ruthless suppression and news management, of appeasement and complicity with Quebec nationalism, came when a TV consortium in charge of the 1994 leaders' debates excluded Equality, despite our seat in the assembly — the first time in modern history that the leader of a party represented in a provincial legislature was denied access to televised debates. The questions of a PQ UDI and Liberal acquiescence, of its constitutional illegality, and of partition or the right to remain Canadian were therefore never highlighted during the election campaign that preceded the October '95 referendum. Citizens went to the polls in ignorance and confusion, unaware of the chaos planned for them by their political and media masters.

The Workings of Local TV News Judgment

by Christy McCormick:
reprinted from The Suburban
September 21, 1993

The following passage is a memo to the CFCF-TV *Pulse News* staff from news director Daniel Freedman:

> First, a warning. This is a howl of outrage...written in the heat of anger. The subject is our irresponsible and unprofessional coverage of the Equality Party....

> The Equality Party is a fringe movement with no future beset by internal problems. It is supported by 6 per cent of the population. But to watch *Pulse News,* you would have a very different impression. Time and again, we have discussed the need to take a more balanced approach by covering the Equality Party in some kind of proportion to its importance. Time and again, we have failed.

> Why this bizarre and inexplicable blind spot? Are we pathologically incapable of exercising routine editorial judgment when it comes to the Equality Party?

On Wednesday, an Equality newser showed up on our air on *Pulse Tonight,* and the item made a comeback the next morning on *Pulse AM.* This, despite the fact that the pitfalls had been discussed at the morning meeting. Meanwhile, other more important stories were not covered. On Friday, Robert Libman showed up in a clip on *Urgence-Santé.* And on Saturday's *Pulse at 6,* we were back at it…yet another Equality Party newser at which nothing new was said. This, despite the fact that the event had been downplayed in the weekend memo. Yet again, other, more important events were not covered (and we had extra cameras to boot.)

The whole situation has become completely intolerable. Fair-minded viewers must wonder if [we] have some kind of axe to grind with this wildly skewed coverage. Our credibility is at risk.

Until now, I have been reluctant to issue draconian edicts. (For every rule there will always be an exception.) I had faith that general guidelines would suffice and staff would act professionally. Sadly, that faith appears to have been misplaced. I am surprised and disappointed in our continued and persistent lapse in professional standards. Clearly, a new approach is needed.

Let's discuss at Tuesday's newsroom meeting. And let's get it right this time…GODAMMIT!…and come up with common sense answers. Otherwise: it's arbitrary edict time. (In the meantime, let's kill the story for *Pulse Tonight.*)

Being a minor expert in media memos, I conclude this has all the hallmarks of the unseen hand from above. The memo is short of examples of what news was missed at the expense of the Equality Party coverage, which suggests more of a distaste for the Equality Party than a preference for anything else.

The memo uses the over-all province-wide figure of 6 percent EP support, rather than the larger figure of 50 percent based on the anglo-media catchment area. That's 6 percent of 7 million Quebecers, or 420,000, and that's more than 50 percent of the 800,000 in anglo-Quebec. Therefore, it is safe to say that EP voters comprise more than half of *Pulse's* 250,000 evening viewers.

One can also see from the memo that Equality coverage is a standing problem, with the staff finding the EP more newsworthy than does the hierarchy. Though there was a reluctance to ban Equality Party news, it was being contemplated. One would think it most odd that an English television station should attack the party which defends its interests. If the Equality Party gains more influence, more people will think that English-speaking community here counts for something more than a dying patient in Canada's palliative care ward. There would be more Toronto media buys of CFCF's advertising time.

But the francophone owners don't seem to care. The whole thing is a triumph of cultural ideology over business sense. I saw it all before at *The Montreal Daily News,* at the hands of Pierre Peladeau, who also owned *Le Journal de Montréal.* He didn't want his *Daily News* to fail, of course, but he insisted that it succeed in the right way. It was to be an anglophone success in terms francophones could accept and control. It didn't work for *The Montreal Daily News* and it won't work for CFCF-12.

The memo makes the unnatural demand that the staff shun news they consider newsworthy and embrace information they care less about. The memo is a denial of a human instinct and will never ring true. But it also shows what the Equality Party is up against at CFCF-12, which has been considered to be fair compared to the hostile CBC.

*T*he following is a letter written to Michael McEwan, Senior Vice-president — Media of the CBC, in which we protested the decision to exclude Equality from the 1994 leadership debate. Our concerns went unheeded and the debate proceeded between Jacques Parizeau and Daniel Johnson alone.

Letter to Michael McEwan — CBC, Vice-President — Media

from Keith Henderson:
August 8, 1994

On August 3, 1994 a media consortium in which CBC is a key participant agreed to a format for the Quebec provincial leaders' debate scheduled tentatively for August 29, 1994. Only two party leaders have been invited, Jacques Parizeau and Daniel Johnson. The leaders of two political parties represented in the legislative assembly of Quebec, the *Parti Action Démocratique* and the Equality Party, which received slightly less than 5% of the popular vote in the last election, were excluded. As the leader of the Equality Party, for whom over 160,000 Quebecers voted in the last election (50 - 60% of the anglophone community by some expert estimates), I find this exclusion bizarre, arbitrary, and morally indefensible.

To begin with, no one in the Equality Party, least of all myself, was apprised that discussions about a leaders' debate were under way. I learned of the prospect through the newspapers and in a letter dated July 26, 1994 and faxed to Pierre Jomphe, *responsable* for the leaders' debate, promptly informed him of the reasons why we felt we should be invited to participate at least in preliminary discussions. The letter went unanswered. Telephone calls to Bruce Kingsley, Micheline Savoie and Claire Samson on and before August 2, 1994 eventually produced an invitation to a meeting with the consortium at 3:30 in the afternoon of August 4. At 9 am August 4, the decision on format (excluding our party) was announced on *Radio Canada's* morning newscast. Why your representatives could not at least have delayed the final decision on format until after hearing our arguments in favour of inclusion remains impossible for me to understand and raises serious questions about the integrity of a process over which the CBC had no small degree of control.

Issues of substance raised by the consortium decision are even more disturbing. These can be dealt with under 3 separate headings — the regulatory history governing the broadcasting of political debates, the special responsibility of public broadcasters to the political process in Canada, and the journalistic considerations surrounding the debate format.

A. *Regulatory History*

Certainly Quebec electoral law foresees the necessity of the presence of the Equality Party in any leaders' debate; Section 423 of the Quebec Election Act reads as follows:

> During an election period, a radio, television or cable broadcaster and the owner of a newspaper, periodical or other publication may make air time on the

radio or television or space in a newspaper, periodical or other publication available free of charge to the leaders of the parties and to candidates, provided he offers such service equitably as to quality and quantity to all the candidates of the same electoral division or to all the leaders of the parties represented in the National Assembly or which obtained at least 3% of the valid votes at the last general election.

Please note that under this act, the Equality Party qualifies for participation under 2 aspects of the law, since the party is represented in the National Assembly and obtained more than 3% of the valid votes in the last election.

The Consortium evidently felt that Quebec Electoral law has no jurisdiction over broadcasters, who come under the regulatory authority of the CRTC. However, the CRTC itself has adopted regulations which govern the holding of public political debates. These regulations set down a number of principles which those responsible for the Consortium ought to have abided by when they pondered whether or not to extend an invitation to the Equality Party to participate:

1. Subsection 3(d) of the Broadcasting Act declares that: "The programming provided by the Canadian broadcasting system should be varied and comprehensive and *should provide reasonable balanced opportunities for the expression of different views on matters of public concern*....

2. During an election period, a licensee shall allocate time for the broadcasting of programs, advertisements on an *equitable basis* to all accredited political parties and such candidates represented in the election...."

3. As noted in the CRTC Circular no. 334: "It is the broadcaster's duty to ensure that the public has adequate knowledge of the issues surrounding an election and the position of the parties and candidates. The broadcaster does not enjoy the position of a benevolent censor who is able to give the public only what it 'should know.' *Nor is it the broadcaster's role to decide in advance which candidates are 'worthy' of broadcast time."*

4. Under Equity in Public Affairs Programming: "In the case of so-called 'debates,' it may be impractical to include all rival parties or candidates in one program. However, if this type of broadcast takes place, *all parties and candidates should be accommodated, even if doing so requires that more than one program be broadcast."*

5. "Licensees who program in more than one language should take into consideration that a political broadcast in one language cannot be construed as balancing a political broadcast in another language."

Responsables for the Consortium may feel that the judgment of Mr. Justice Borins of the Ontario Court (recently upheld by the Supreme Court) has rendered the principles outlined above legally unenforceable, however it is the view of the Equality Party that while the legal enforceability of these principles may now be in doubt (pending stricter wording of Election Broadcasting Regulations by the CRTC), the *moral* value of both the Quebec Election Act and the regulations of the CRTC remains unimpeachable. How a public broadcaster like the CBC can allow itself to ignore both the spirit of the law and 15 years of solid regulatory interpretive history simply because the CRTC has not worded its enabling regulation correctly is beyond my comprehension.

B. Responsibility of Broadcasters to the Political Process in Canada

Were the Consortium to proceed with its contemplated exclusion of the Equality Party, the Consortium (*and* the CBC) would be establishing a unenviable broadcasting precedent in Canada — the first time in modern history (to my understanding) that leaders of political parties represented in a provincial assembly would have been excluded from a debate. I remind you of two recent examples in New Brunswick and in British Columbia. The New Brunswick debates included *four* parties, 3 of them *without any seats in the legislature.* A previously unknown party, COR, emerged from the debates and the subsequent election as the official opposition. In B.C., the leader of the provincial Liberal party was allowed to participate in a debate even though his party had no seats in the legislature. He emerged from the debate and the subsequent election as the leader of the opposition. It might be useful to remind those responsible for the Consortium that under the format contemplated, Preston Manning, Audrey McLaughlin or Lucien Bouchard would not have been permitted to participate in the federal election debates during the fall of 1993. Those debates would have occurred between two parties only, one of which was later reduced to only 2 seats in the House of Commons. (Moreover those debates would have occurred in English only.) Canada does not operate according to a two party system. It is a betrayal of the principles of Parliament to try to impose a two-party model through arbitrary broadcast debate formats during an election period. Our system contemplates the possibility of minority governments, i.e. large political formations governing with the support of smaller ones. To exclude smaller parties from the important debate process simply because they are small curtails the possibility of them becoming larger in the future and unconscionably reduces the scope and suppleness of what was intended in a healthy multi-party democracy.

C. A Less than Fertile Debate

Those who decided to exclude the Equality Party claim they were doing so based on 'journalistic considerations.' "People want to hear from parties that might form a government," is the argument most often heard, but decision-makers at CBC should be reminded that Lucien Bouchard could not form a government in 1993 because his party presented candidates only in Quebec, yet he was permitted to debate. It should also be pointed out that at this crucial stage in Quebec's history (and Canada's as well), in this election characterized by at least one of the key participants as a 'referendum-election,' the two major provincial parties actually *agree* on 3 matters of great significance. Parizeau and Johnson agree that a referendum victory based on 50% + 1 of the Quebec electorate is sufficient to take Quebec out of Canada. Only the Equality Party among parties represented in the Assembly disagrees with both the tool and the number. Parizeau and Johnson agree that the decision about Quebec's future in Canada is one for Quebec alone to decide. Only the Equality Party believes that Quebec cannot secede from Canada without Canada's consent. Parizeau and Johnson agree that should Quebec separate it may do so with its borders intact. Only the Equality Party believes that in the event of separation, strongly Canadian regions of Quebec should be able to choose what state they wished to be governed by, just as the Cree were promised the choice by the federal Minister of Native Affairs, and so the question of why Canada's borders are negotiable but Quebec's borders are "inviolable" needs to be discussed. In short, the elimination of the Equality Party from the projected debate eliminates a major strain of public opinion, one shared (at least in part) by many Quebecers and many other Canadians too. Why should such a debate be so impoverished?

Please understand that it is not the position of the Equality Party to seek legal injunctions against a debate that we believe ought to take place, nor is it the position of the party that equal time need be given to all participants. What we are protesting is the arbitrary dismissal of 15 years broadcasting code on the subject and the outright exclusion of our ideas. We hope that you are in a position to prevent such an unfortunate precedent from being set.

*I*n the September 1994 elections, though the PQ and the Liberals virtually tied in terms of popular vote, notorious skewing of the Quebec electoral map in favour of rural ridings gave the separatists a substantial majority. The Equality Party was wiped off the map. What follows is a press communiqué issued the night of that defeat.

Referendum Debate Will Vindicate Equality's Ideas

Press Communiqué:
September 15, 1994

Despite Monday's election defeat, the Equality Party will be vindicated as its ideas and principles take center stage in the Quebec referendum debate, EP leader Keith Henderson said last night. "I know we're going to be vindicated. The arguments we've raised may be a little premature," he said. "People haven't quite cottoned on to their significance, and that was because we neither did the job of explaining well enough, nor received sufficient opportunity to explain well enough to voters. But you'll see what we've been saying all along will be front and center in the Canadian agenda."

Mr. Henderson said EP failed to win a seat because its arguments "have been a bit too far ahead of our own clientele. But I'm sure they'll see. They'll quickly catch up." He said Equality could not surmount the fear campaign that its opponents waged against anglophone voters. "The *Parti Québécois'* separation threats sufficiently frightened strong-minded Canadians here. They felt there was better strength in numbers with the Liberals, even though they're weak federalists, than with articulate but less numerous Equality members. The irony is that most voters support our principles.

Brent Tyler, EP candidate in Westmount-St.-Louis, said the Liberals "did so well against us because they were successful in their fear-mongering strategy. People voted out of fear, not principle.... Let's see what kind of opposition to the PQ [victorious Liberal opponent] Jacques Chagnon can mount in Quebec City. Then voters can re-assess things."

Mr. Henderson criticized past and present federal government silence for abetting fears. "In the absence of a statement from the federal government, people feel frightened that they don't have a protector and that they don't have choices available to them. So I blame the federal government for its silence on this fundamental issue. We've been living for 25 years with a threat that deforms and reduces political debate. Take that threat away, and people will consider options, nuances, and differences between parties. With it, they won't."

Mr. Henderson said Equality was hurt by past internal splits and the excessive attention given them. "Rifts occur in all young parties trying to define themselves, and we picked the crucible of the [1992] Charlottetown Accord, where all of Canada was wrestling with a major and divisive issue, to define ourselves," he added, referring to the subsequent defections of two Equality MNAs. Said Mr. Tyler, "Every party has its baggage. It's amazing the Liberals survived their baggage of helping to found the *Bloc Québécois* and having the Jean Allaire-Mario

Dumont contingent leave the party." He said Equality was more affected by defections because it was a smaller party.

On Equality's future, Mr. Henderson said his party will forge ahead, advancing its principles in an extra-parliamentary manner, such as presenting a complaint over Quebec's discriminatory English school access laws to the United Nations. He said EP may seek allies outside Quebec. "For now, we'll find much stronger support for our views from other Canadians, who can be persuaded to help Canadians inside Quebec, than we will from our own clientele." Reflecting the tenacity that distinguished his campaign, Mr. Henderson told supporters that the fight had just begun. "We're not going to abandon our principles ever. We're going to be there year after year, and you'll see that just as a surprise happened in 1989, another surprise will happen in the future. Just keep the faith and stay united. We'll persist. And persistence in Canadian politics is a real virtue."

"A la prochaine fois."

The Struggle Against UDI

Quebec Referendum 1995

*T*he 'extra-parliamentary' means Equality chose to advance its agenda was the Special Committee for Canadian Unity, *brainchild of Stephen Scott and grandfather of the Unity Movement that sprang up during and after the '95 referendum. The SCCU was non-partisan, in that it accepted membership from any organization that shared its aims, but since those aims included the stated preference for an indivisible Canada, the establishment by the Courts that a Quebec UDI was unconstitutional, and the territorial division of Quebec in the event of negotiated secession, Equality felt very much at home. Our first major initiative was a January '95 press conference in which we announced, in the words of the* Toronto Star, *that "many Quebecers ... won't comply with this unconstitutional and illegal law" and that we would be taking the* Draft Bill on the Sovereignty of Quebec *to court. In separatist circles, the press conference provoked no small degree of consternation. Consistent with the vacuity and evasiveness of Quebec Liberal party policy on the matter, Daniel Johnson responded only by saying he had no intention of waging "judicial guerilla warfare" against the PQ. Separatist Ed Bantey opened the charge by suggesting Scott's dismissal from his McGill law faculty job.*

The Bourgault Affair

by Ed Bantey:
reprinted from the Gazette
January 22, 1995

The fuss over Pierre Bourgault's "ominous" warning about the consequences of a massive non-francophone NO to sovereignty illustrates how selective a memory some people have. While federalist tenors, both English- and French-speaking, demanded that Premier Jacques Parizeau fire Bourgault for uttering "threats" of violence (which he didn't, by the way), they seem not to notice repeated threats (blunt and direct) from their own camp.

Did anyone hear federalists protesting, for example, when a belligerent Professor Stephen Scott of McGill University argued for the use of armed force to stop Quebec from seceding if — horror of horror — a majority of Quebecers vote YES? The constitutional-law specialist has been sabre-rattling for years, as have many armchair generals. That's different, you say? Scott, unlike Bourgault, isn't on the public payroll?

Wrong. As a professor, he costs Quebecers — including the sovereignists he wants to crush — a lot more than the fees Bourgault would have collected as a part-time consultant to Parizeau. And Scott is by no means alone in trying to lay the groundwork for armed repression in the event Quebecers vote democratically to separate. All that talk of illegality emanating from Prime Minister Jean Chrétien and other federalists is nothing if not a threat.

It will be claimed that Chrétien and others who harp on illegality aren't suggesting violent means, that they're talking constitutional law. It could be argued — as separatist loose-cannon Guy Bertrand does for reasons best known to himself — that a YES vote wouldn't stand the test of a court challenge.

Let's assume Chrétien and Bertrand are right, that the courts would deny Quebecers the right to sovereignty, no matter what a majority might decide. What then? What if the Quebec government follows the sovereign will of Quebecers and proceeds with a declaration of independence despite the courts? How could Ottawa enforce the court ruling without resorting to force, without sending in the armed forces, to quell what would then be, in the legal sense, an act of rebellion? That, it seems to me, is more "ominous" a threat than Bourgault's "dangerous situation" remark. Yet federalists don't demand Chrétien's resignation or Scott's dismissal when they trot out the illegality time-bomb. And sovereignists don't denounce Chrétien or Scott as racists because they, directly or indirectly, justify the use of force to keep largely French-speaking Quebec from pulling out.

Bourgault admits he goofed, but put his convictions ahead of his personal ambitions by resigning to spare Parizeau embarrassment. But some federalists complain that the premier didn't tar and feather Bourgault as well.

The truth, of course, is that *l'affaire Bourgault* was an attempted Yvette coup that failed. The English-language media blew it out of proportion in the hope that it would make the kind of wave Lise Payette did with the remark about Yvettes prior to the 1980 referendum on sovereignty-association. That gaffe was used very skilfully by federalists to mobilize women for the NO side.

Federalists need a new Yvette incident to light up the flat NO campaign, but Parizeau and Bourgault acted quickly to deprive them of the *cause célèbre* that seemed within reach. Since *l'affaire Bourgault* didn't fly, tune in next week — and each week after that until the referendum — for a new Yvette scenario....

Referendum Provides Impressive Façade for Dictatorial *Coup d'État*

by Keith Henderson:
Gazette *Letters*
January 29, 1995

I n the quirky world of Quebec separatists, it seems now that to advocate the rule of law over the right to secession is to become a sabre-rattling racist. If you happen to be a respected constitutional lawyer at a Quebec university, like McGill's Stephen Scott, it is only fair and decent that, since the Quebec government is paying your salary, and you are speaking against the Quebec government, you should be fired.

Why? In the world according to Ed Bantey, every ethnic or linguistic group (such as "the largely French-speaking Quebec") has an inherent right to secede from democratically established federations — no matter how successful and this despite whatever the courts may say. (At least 3000 separate ethno-linguistic groups exist in other countries. Should all of them become separate states?) For separatists and their federalist fellow-travellers, any province so desiring may conduct a referendum, win it by as small a margin as 50% + 1 ("a win is a win" to quote opposition leader Daniel Johnson), and declare independence unilaterally. Other Canadians might want a word to say about this destruction of their country, but they don't count. Canadians inside Quebec might resent being cut off from their heritage and birthright. Too bad for them. Canada's negotiable; Quebec's indivisible. The only way to stop the process, as Bantey quite wrongly suggests, is to use force — then Canada will be the aggressor and who is prepared to live with that?

Bantey, of course, doesn't mention that after the legislative rebellion of UDI, in order to compel loyal Canadians to pay all their taxes to Quebec City, Parizeau will have to use the courts and the police — i.e. force, "the original sin of government," to quote that 'sabre-rattling racist' of Bantey's own special demonology, Stephen Scott. But in the weird solipsistic world of separatists, we can assume 'that's alright for us, but not for you.'

Turmoil, chaos, competing legitimacies, political tragedy, not to mention the firing of dissenting voices and a dropping dollar — that is what awaits Canadians should we abandon the rule of law, follow Bantey and Parizeau's siren call to direct provincial plebiscitory democracy, and put our country at risk every 10 or 15 years until separatists get the vote they want. No provincial government in Canada can simply and arbitrarily write its own rules, conduct referendums, then act illegally on the results. That way lies chaos.

"The dictators of this century, following the example of Napoleon, have in turn relied upon such referendums or plebiscites for legitimizing their unconstitutional and anticonstitutional regimes. Such direct popular approval provides an impressive façade for the dictatorial *coup d'état* and can be used against democratic opposition at home and abroad on the pretence that the 'will of the people' has been consulted," wrote Professor Carl J. Friederich in the book *Constitutional Government and Democracy*.

That warning is immensely salutary for Canadians.

Let's Not Get Excited

by Guy Laforest:
reprinted from Le Devoir
February 17, 1995

In the great book of the [1995] pre-referendum campaign, the time has come for alarmist scenarios. In 1980, that chapter was dedicated to economic matters. This time, the tone is more serious. People are raising the spectre of civil disobedience, if not armed resistance. Furious over losing their country, Canadians inside Quebec won't stand for it; they're reacting. What is one to make of it all?

Within the range of destinies open to societies, the worst case scenario always remains a possibility. One can hardly dismiss it out of hand. However, as my colleague Jean-Pierre Derriennic in his book on Quebec independence has underscored, crack-ups can occur without the people involved really wanting them to, if a certain number of preconditions come together.

If the tone has been raised a notch or two over 15 years, it is first of all because, this time, the sovereignist option has a real chance of winning. In 1980, we were still in the age of innocence, of amateurism. We were still going to school. In 1995, we can't afford to fail our final exams.

Without doubt, public rumblings are sending out signals that force us to pay attention to the alarmist scenarios. Keith Henderson, leader of the Equality Party, has declared that sovereignty would be the equivalent of a dictatorial *coup d'état*. Stephen Scott, professor of law at McGill, affirms that the secession of Quebec would be illegal and revolutionary and invites the federal government to have the army intervene to re-establish order. William Johnson has furnished a coherent thesis to this little school of thought by reducing the history of modern Quebec to that of an ethnic anglophobe state. When we see photographs where professor Scott is seated at the same table as Doctor Singh, head Canadian nationalist among the cultural communities of Montreal, and Mohawk leader Joe Norton, we can only conclude these people are meeting each other to cook something up.

These, then, are the people in Quebec whose talk has fed the risks of a crack-up, the sort of thing that can happen in a place like Montreal where language and at times racial cleavages are deepened by a high level of poverty and urban disaffection. Not to mention the alienation that is currently ravaging the aboriginal communities. Extremist talk on one side, difficult social conditions on the other. Is that enough for us to get nervous about? Yes and no.

The worst case scenarios cobbled together in Quebec in 1995 all rely on the following premise: given a narrow sovereignist referendum victory,

Canada and the federal government will dig in their heels and will refuse to negotiate (or they will be incapable of doing so, another variation on the same theme), thus forcing the Quebec government to declare independence unilaterally. For a certain period of time, two legal systems, two legitimacies will clash on Quebec territory, opening the breach for all kinds of disputes and potential crack-ups. The absence of a legal adjudication process risks plunging our society into chaos.

I feel compelled to say that the prophets of the apocalypse will be disappointed. For an English Canadian expert, originally from Quebec, has just demonstrated the utter fragility of these mechanisms of catastrophe. Robert Young is a professor of political science at Western. He has just completed a lengthy term at the Institute of Intergovernmental Relations in Kingston at Queen's. This institute is renowned for its close relations with the federal mandarinate and the Canadian government. Robert Young's book, *The Secession of Quebec and the Future of Canada,* which recently appeared off the presses of McGill-Queen's, with a translation due in April from Laval University Press, is the most detailed, the most exhaustive study available on the dynamics of Quebec secession and its transition toward sovereignty. Everything is covered. The debt, monetary policy, the fate of aboriginal peoples, the scope and nature of negotiations. The book will quickly become incontrovertible. I will restrict myself to outlining certain of the author's conclusions.

If sovereignists win the referendum, even by a narrow margin, Young believes the federal government will have no other choice but to sit down and negotiate. In any other eventuality, the weight of political and economic uncertainty will become simply intolerable. They won't negotiate with a light heart. But they will nevertheless negotiate.

Daniel Johnson and Michel Bélanger will jump all of a sudden when they see how Young demolishes the arguments of those who think Canada will collapse into impotence the day after a referendum won by the sovereignists. The shock of a YES vote will create, beyond the initial surprise, an immense wave of solidarity in the rest of Canada, the principal beneficiary of which will be the federal government. The latter will very quickly set a negotiating committee to work, one in which opposition parties and provincial governments will have to be represented. According to Young, the hypothesis of unilateral action by Quebec is highly unlikely.

The Quebec government would be wrong, however, to become too reassured by this book. In order for the transition process to be civilized, it will be necessary to impose on all sovereignist leading lights a certain language of respect and partnership toward the rest of Canada. It will be necessary as well to win the confidence of anglophones and aboriginals by offering them specific guarantees. Before the referendum. Finally, it will be necessary during the month of March [1995] to give the National Assembly all the latitude needed to improve the *Draft Bill on the Sovereignty of Quebec.* Our common future must be mapped out in an atmosphere of calm and without undue haste.

Strange Extremists!

by Keith Henderson:
reprinted from Le Devoir
March 15, 1995

A lways with the aim of characterizing the arguments of his adversaries as extreme, alarmist, even violent, Guy Laforest has accused me not only of declaring that "sovereignty would be the equivalent of a dictatorial *coup d'état,"* but of having recently sat down beside professor of constitutional law, Stephen Scott, Dr. Roopnarine Singh, and Kanawake Grand Chief Joe Norton in order to "cook something up."

To begin with, I want to remind Mr. Laforest just what these 'things' are we've been cooking up in the Special Committee for Canadian Unity — going before the country's courts, should ever Mr. Parizeau adopt the *Draft Bill on the Sovereignty of Quebec,* to determine whether or not the Bill is constitutional. Strange kind of violent extremists who want to proceed via the route of the Canadian judiciary. Can one say as much of Messieurs Laforest and Parizeau? Are they ready to put the problem of the legality of the *Draft Bill* before the courts straightaway so we can assure the population of Quebec that the referendum proposal already prepared by their government is legal and constitutional?

Let's recall it was precisely judicial recourse (before Quebec courts) that René Lévesque sought in 1981 when he wanted to question the constitutionality of Trudeau's initiatives. Lévesque lost. Mr. Parizeau seems to prefer the path of unilateralism and illegality. Who, then, is the extremist?

Secondly, I have never argued that the sovereignty of Quebec would be the "equivalent of a dictatorial *coup d'état.*" Like professor Scott and a number of other Canadian commentators, including Mr. Laforest's colleague, Jean-Pierre Derriennic, I said that sovereignty, self-proclaimed by the National Assembly, without the consent of its Canadian partners, would be the equivalent of a dictatorial *coup d'état.* The difference is crucial.

It is in this context that I took the opportunity to cite the salutary warning of political scientist Carl J. Friedrich who, in his book *Constitutional Government and Democracy,* came to the following conclusion: the dictators of the twentieth century, inspired by Napoleon, often resorted to the instrument of referendums in order to legitimize their unconstitutional régimes, because such direct popular support furnished "an impressive façade for a dictatorial *coup d'état.*" Holding referendums like provincial opinion polls is not beyond the law in Canada. Attempting to replace the constitution of Canada by provincial referendums, that's a *coup d'état.* That is dictatorship.

I would take the opportunity as well to offer Mr. Laforest my sincere hopes that given a victory by the YES of a sufficient majority, negotiations between the government of Quebec and the rest of Canada will begin quickly. Nevertheless, I would remind him of two things which seem self-evident to me but which might not be clear to our separatist co-citizens. Despite the recent arguments of Western professor of political science, Robert Young, according to whom "the federal government will rapidly set up a negotiating committee," one should never minimize the difficulties a YES vote will create (especially if that victory is a narrow one) and the possibility of a profound inertia on the part of the rest of Canada. Secondly, one should never fool the population by pretending that these negotiations (if they ever occur) would prevent a unilateral declaration of independence by the Quebec government — an illegal and anti-constitutional declaration. The *Draft Bill* clearly and unequivocally stipulates that Section 1 declaring Quebec a sovereign country "will come into effect one year after its approval by referendum." The *Draft Bill* doesn't say that the law would come into effect only if the National Assembly is convinced negotiations already undertaken had borne fruit. The law and the declaration of independence will come into effect — period.

Therefore, the Parizeau YES is not at all, as messieurs Young and Laforest have argued, an instrument to force negotiations to occur, as was the case for the Lévesque YES in 1980. The Parizeau YES is decisive, heavy with harmful legal consequences, anti-constitutional, and destructive of the rule of law essential for the preservation of peace, order, and

good government in Canada. And we're the extremists?

*O*n March 3, 1995 Equality delivered the following brief to the Parti Québécois' Commission on the Future of Quebec. Daniel Johnson's artful Quebec Liberal Party dodged the hearings, claiming that their presence would simply provide legitimacy to a propaganda charade. Our view was that the Quebec Liberals didn't want to face the PQ in open debate over a UDI and risk revealing to the staunchly Canadian wing of their electorate how weak and conditional their commitment to Canada and its constitution really was.

Anarchy, Discord, Miscreancy & Ruin

by Keith Henderson:
Brief submitted to the Commission on the Future of Quebec

1. The Rule of Law

The evolution of western democracies, from *Magna Carta* onward, is fixed on two political centres of gravity, two principles, each orbiting the other, each distinct and different. The first of these is government by the people and of the people. It implies that issues affecting citizens within a given jurisdiction are determined electorally by the majority within that jurisdiction, either by referendum or through the people's representatives. The second is government by the rule of law. It implies that the principle of majority rule must be qualified — and qualified fundamentally and unimpeachably — by laws which a given majority can neither ignore nor lightly overturn, laws which, taken together, we call the Constitution. I welcome the opportunity to remind the representatives of the government of Quebec, embarked on a course unprecedented in Canadian history of trivializing and jettisoning the fundamental rule of law in our land, just why their proposals are flawed and wrong, inconsistent with our Canadian traditions and international law, and inimical to the spirit of democracy.

In western democratic federations, among which Canada has long and honourably numbered, the rule of law takes precedence over the will of the majority, either national or local, in at least three important ways. It is the constitution, not the majority, that determines the boundaries of a given jurisdiction. It is the constitution, not the majority, that separates issues affecting and therefore properly decided by *all* the people from issues affecting and therefore properly decided by some. Finally, it is the constitution, not the majority, that determines which issues can be decided by single legislatures and which cannot.

Constitution, not majority, determines boundaries

In Canada, the administrative territories of the nation are determined by the constitution, not by any single legislature. The Parliament of Canada cannot attach the city of Hull to Ontario. Neither can the government of Quebec annex the territory of Labrador. The constitution forbids it. Nor can a province, by an act of its own legislature, unilaterally secede from Confederation and so permanently alter the boundaries of the country. Those who pretend that Canada's constitution is silent on this matter are wrong. Only an amendment to the *Constitution Acts 1867 to 1982* can achieve this change, and such an amendment will require the participation and approval of *all* Canadians, since it is the country of all Canadians that will be affected. As the *Globe and Mail* wrote: "Every citizen of this country is a citizen of the whole of this country, and should not be expected to stand and watch while a part of it is wrenched away."

Constitution, not majority, separates issues affecting all from issues affecting some

In Canada, sections 91 and 92 of the *British North America Act* determine which classes of law may be adopted by the national government and which by the provincial government. Those who argue that the constitution is irrelevant or meaningless or somehow void in this regard because not consented to by the National Assembly are wrong. A century ago Sir John A. MacDonald found it was illegal for the federal Parliament to regulate the sale of liquor in this country. It remains illegal for the federal government to do so. Five years ago Robert Bourassa found it was illegal for the government of Quebec to regulate telecommunications in Canada. It remains illegal for it to do so. Section 1 of the *Draft Bill on the Sovereignty of Quebec* declares that "Quebec is a sovereign country" and therefore purports to expand the classes of acts under which the province of Quebec may legislate to include *all* acts — the classic definition of sovereignty. Section 1 of the *Draft Bill,* as interpreted in the Quebec government's *Guide to Participation in the Commissions on the Future of Quebec,* also proposes to expel from the territory of Quebec all taxation authority of the federal government. Thus the legal proposition that "Quebec is a sovereign country" represents an expansion of the authority of the legislature of Quebec and a corresponding expulsion of the authority of the Parliament of Canada which only the constitution of Canada, not the National Assembly, has the right to accomplish. Section 51 of *The Constitution Acts 1867 to 1982* reads: "The Constitution of Canada is the supreme law of Canada, and any law that is inconsistent with the provisions of the Constitution is, to the extent of the inconsistency, of no force or effect." If enacted by the government of Quebec in its present form, the *Draft Bill on the Sovereignty of Quebec* will be inconsistent with the Constitution of Canada, therefore illegal, null and void.

Constitution, not majority, determines which issues can be decided by legislatures

Thirdly, in Canada, the constitution, not a single legislature, determines what laws can be legally adopted and which cannot. The legislative majority in the province of Quebec, for example, cannot enforce a law banning the practice of a certain religion, regardless of whether a majority of residents in the province approves of such a law, and regardless of whether that approval has been sought in a referendum. Canada's constitution forbids the adoption of such laws. By the same token, whether supported by a majority of residents in Quebec or not, in a referendum or not, the legislature of Quebec cannot unilaterally determine, as the *Draft Bill* suggests, that the "Court of Appeal of Quebec shall become the court of highest jurisdiction" in Quebec, when the Constitution of Canada has determined that the court of highest jurisdiction, for the residents of Quebec as for all Canadians, is the Supreme Court of Canada. Nor can the legislature of Quebec, whether approved by a referendum or not, unilaterally declare Quebec a sovereign country. Some laws can be passed by simple majorities in legislatures. Others require the operation of the amending formula to take effect. Quebec's accession to the status of an independent country will affect a host of constitutional provisions in Canada. There can be no doubt that for the government's *Draft Bill* to succeed, and to avoid the catastrophe of rebellion, the government will have to secure an amendment to the Constitution, section 52 (3) of which reads: "Amendments to the Constitution of Canada shall be made only in accordance with the authority contained in the Constitution of Canada." That authority does not confer upon provincial governments the power to pass laws like the *Draft Bill on the Sovereignty of Quebec,* conduct referendums to give those laws force and effect, and then act illegally on the results.

To pretend otherwise, to assert that all legislative matters in the state reduce themselves merely to political questions and the simple exercise of majority rule in jurisdictions that may represent the tiniest fraction of the population as a whole, is to betray a profound ignorance of the way in which mature democracies function. It is to subordinate the constitution to transient passions and expediencies, to unbalance what is finely tuned, to explode the federal nature of the country. It is to countenance revolution. It is finally, carelessly, and in our view tragically, to invite the anarchy, discord, miscreancy and ruin, evident in other places and times and from which Canada has blessedly been spared.

2. *The Right to Secede*

M embers of the government of Quebec and their supporters have often invoked the principle of self-determination of peoples to buttress their contention that the province of Quebec has the inherent right to secede from Canada. However, as the cabinet ministers who prepared the *Draft Bill on the Sovereignty of Quebec* were well aware, in international law the right to self-determination confers upon Quebec no corresponding right to secession.

In May of 1992, five distinguished experts in international law testified before the Bélanger-Campeau Commission's *Sovereignty Committee.* They said the following:

> The right of peoples to self-determination is a very general principle, which has as a consequence always and everywhere the right for the community involved to participate in its future, but this does not suffice to provide a basis for the right of a people to accede to independence, to the detriment of the state to which it is attached, except in colonial situations....

> ...One cannot reasonably maintain that [Quebec] is a colonial people, nor that it is deprived of the right to its own existence within the Canadian whole, nor to participate in democratic life.... And therefore the Quebec people effectively exercises its right to self-determination within the framework of the Canadian whole and is not legally well-founded to invoke it to justify a future accession to independence....

> ...The right to secession does not exist in international law.... The generalization of the right to self-determination, understood as the right for a people to es-

tablish a state, would have dramatically destabiliz-
ing effects, which obviously cannot be countenanced
by an international society made up in the first place
of sovereign States.

We can therefore safely conclude that the
government's *Draft Bill on the Sovereignty of Quebec*
can claim no support whatsoever under international law.

Shorn of legal trappings for justification, government supporters have reverted to political analogies to support their arguments, ranging from the
American Declaration of Independence upon which
the premier has said Quebec's *Declaration of Sovereignty* will be modelled, to examples drawn from the
ferment of post-communist Europe. "No legal basis
existed for the emergence of new European states,"
this argument goes, "but that hasn't prevented the
international community from recognizing them."
From this perspective, what legitimizes secession is
international recognition, not international law,
hence the visits of our peripatetic premier to France,
the United States, accompanied by as much pomp
and circumstance as Quebec representatives can so-
licit from their hosts. Two caveats should be borne
in mind, however, by those who seek to legitimize
unilateral and revolutionary secession through international recognition.

3. Caveat Emptor

No recognition without just cause

First, as professor of political science at U of T, David Cameron has pointed out, the American revolutionaries, aware "that governments long established should not be changed for light and transient causes," took it upon themselves to "declare the causes which impel[led] them to separation." These included the British monarch's refusal to hold elections, the denial of trial by jury, and the waging of war against the people.

> What causes of separation are offered by the government of Quebec to satisfy "a decent respect to the opinions of mankind?" In all the documents placed before the National Assembly earlier this month at this solemn moment in the history of the people of Quebec, only one cause of separation is mentioned: "to settle definitively the constitutional problem that has been confronting Quebec for several generations." No allegations of tyranny, no abuse of power, no denial of democratic rights, no confiscation of property, no infringement on the liberties of the citizen. Just a "constitutional problem."

More egregiously misleading still are analogies to the emergence of new states in Eastern Europe. The Constitution of the Soviet Union, more honoured in the breach than the observance, nevertheless explicitly provided for the secession of constituent republics, many forcibly annexed to the Soviet Union earlier this century, many with a prior history of independent nationhood, many having suffered unspeakably under Soviet domination, the millions of victims of the 1933 famine in Ukraine being the most notable example. None of these conditions even remotely pertains to Quebec. Quebec was not an independent country when its territory *as a province* was officially defined by the BNA Act of 1867. There are no provisions for secession in our constitution. There is no appreciable history of violence or tyrannical oppression in Canada to justify secession. In fact, as professor Cameron has pointed out, Quebecers...

> are unquestionably living in one of the freest countries on the face of the globe, protected by the rule of law, an independent judiciary and a constitutional Charter of Rights.... The vast majority of francophones in Canada live within Quebec, where they make up more than 80 per cent of the population. Enjoying the benefits of what is arguably the most decentralized federal system on the globe, their government is free to fashion very much the kind of society that the majority wants — in health care, in education, in social policy, in the structure of the economy and, to a substantial degree, in immigration.... This is tyranny?

Apart from a few mischievous and hypocritical politicians in France, whose constitution contains an indivisibility clause rendering the aspirations of their own Basque and Corsican separatists legally void, it is difficult to imagine other G7 nations offering any recognition to Quebec's self-proclaimed independence, in the absence of both just cause and Canadian consent.

International recognition requires expulsion of Canadian law

Secondly, separatists in the government of Quebec should recall the criteria the American State Department has established for recognition of breakaway states. No one would argue that American recognition will not be crucial to the success of the *Draft Bill,* revolutionary and illegal under both Canadian and international law as it is. For a break-away state to secure recognition, it must demonstrate effective control over the territory it claims to administer, *i.e.* it must expel from its territory the application of all other authorities, in this case that of the Parliament of Canada. In the opinion of Patrick J. Monahan in his study for the C.D. Howe Institute, "It seems inconceivable that Canada would simply acquiesce in a Quebec UDI. Rather than accept Quebec's unilateral declaration as a *fait accompli,* Canadian leaders would contest its validity and attempt to force the Quebec government to back down." This in turn would provoke what Monahan calls "a disastrous contest for supremacy" in which "two rival governments would be competing for supremacy over the territory of Quebec," with no certainty of outcome apart from the creation of "a constitutional, political, and economic crisis the likes of which Canadians have never seen."

4. The Consequences of Illegal Acts

Law-abiding citizens are under no compulsion to obey illegal acts

Should the government of Quebec nevertheless persist in its reckless course, a host of objectionable consequences will follow. The cabinet will surely have considered the intolerable dilemma in which a referendum victory and illegal UDI would plunge law-abiding citizens in Quebec. Administrators — of cegeps, hospitals, businesses large and small — may choose to continue remitting taxes to Ottawa *despite* directives from Quebec to the contrary. What would happen if citizens refused to obey these directives? What law would take precedence? Would the government of Quebec use force (i.e. the courts and the police) to compel Quebecers to obey the laws of its revolutionary régime? Would the government of Quebec interfere with the day to day activities of the many federal employees on its territory — customs agents, RCMP officers, members of the military — in order to oblige them to obey *their* orders and not Ottawa's? What would the government do with judges on the bench who continued to recognize the primacy of Canadian law? How would the Quebec government impound federal taxes to prevent its full share of Canada's debt from being paid, as it has at times threatened to do?

Thus far only former PQ party whip and constitutional spokesman Jacques Brassard has pronounced himself on this subject, stating that an independent Quebec *would* use every means of authority available to it, including force, to compel Quebecers to obey its laws. "Quebec would have to use its full authority," M. Brassard said on May 31, 1994 to a *Presse Canadienne* reporter, "and that means the law, the courts, and the police force, which are also institutions, instruments of the state." If M. Brassard's views represent those of the government of Quebec, it behooves the government to say so, now, before conducting a referendum on the subject, so Quebecers can know the full gravity of the proposal their provincial government intends to put before them, *i.e.* that the *Draft Bill on the Sovereignty of Quebec* is illegal and the government is aware of its illegality, that the National Assembly has no power either to adopt or enforce it, whether supported by referendum or not, and the government is aware of that fact, that the government of Quebec nevertheless intends, consciously and deliberately, to engage in an assault against the Constitution of Canada, to engage itself in illegal activities, and to engage the National Assembly of this province in the perpetration of a *coup d'état*. Such a course of action is not astute; it is rank folly. Even government supporters, like Guy Bertrand who once ran for the leadership of the *Parti Québécois,* recognize this. "I have concluded," said M. Bertrand, "like many sovereignist Quebecers or nationalists, that the question as posed in the *Draft Bill on the Sovereignty of Quebec* risks becoming a suicidal adventure." Law-abiding Canadian-minded citizens of this province will tolerate neither such acts nor the procedures which engendered them. Speaking personally, and on behalf of the Equality Party I represent, I am here today to tell you — solemnly, serenely, and supported by the full vigour of Canadian law — that we will obey only those laws that the Constitution of Canada sanctions and no others. The laws of a revolutionary, self-proclaimed government of an independent Quebec, the laws envisaged in *The Draft Bill on the Sovereignty of Quebec* we will not obey. Those laws will have no legitimacy, neither in our consciences, in our hearts, nor in fact. Those laws should never be adopted. They should never even be proposed.

Referendums cannot replace Constitution

Refusal to obey illegal laws does not equate to refusing the government of Quebec its right to conduct referendums. Quebec is entitled to conduct whatever referendum it wishes, including, of course, the 1980 referendum where René Lévesque requested the people to provide their provincial government with a mandate to negotiate sovereignty-association, a request the people rejected. However that referendum bore no constitutional consequences, whether won or lost, and the request for a mandate to negotiate pre-supposed the necessity of obtaining Canadian agreement to whatever the government managed to secure. The referendum proposed by the *Draft Bill on the Sovereignty of Quebec* bears no resemblance whatever to the referendum of 1980. The *Draft Bill* invests the proposed referendum with the power to give force and effect to legislation which only the Constitution of Canada is empowered to do, *i.e.* the *Draft Bill* invests the proposed referendum (illegally) with powers that supersede the amending formula.

Those who argue that the independence of Quebec is strictly a political matter should therefore demand, as we do, that the government of Quebec, if it insists of its separatist agenda, return to the methods laid out by Lévesque, sever the proposed referendum and the *Draft Bill* of any constitutional implications whatever, and simply poll Quebecers (if poll it must) on whether they want independence from Canada. Should a substantial majority say yes, that will merely begin the arduous democratic process of negotiated break-up, with all its attendant stresses, difficulties, and required approvals, and with no guarantee of success. Should the majority say no, as is likely, the government of Quebec would be well advised to desist finally from its divisive and debilitating régime and seek the amendments to the Constitution it wishes through more conventional means. Canadians have had more than enough of referendums.

Governments must refer the Draft Bill on the Sovereignty of Quebec to the courts

If the government remains unconvinced by these arguments and those advanced by constitutional experts, by the Prime Minister and by the federal Minister of Justice, that the *Draft Bill on the Sovereignty of Quebec* is illegal and unconstitutional, let it do the proper thing under Canadian law and refer the matter to the courts straightaway. Democracy demands that voters be informed, not by legislators but by the judiciary, whether a course of action proposed by their government is legal or illegal. It is the sworn duty of legislators to uphold the constitution and the rule of law in Canada. The government of Quebec must not be party to submitting illegal acts to the population for their endorsement, to ask what cannot be given and sanction what cannot be approved. Our firm counsel to the government is to seek a judgment before it proceeds one step further down the path it has chosen. It is within its power to do so. It is its duty to do so. Should it shirk that duty and should federal leaders assist it in that course of irresponsibility, by not referring the matter themselves or using their power of veto to disallow illegal acts in provincial legislatures, the Equality Party, together with other concerned citizens, will attempt to defend the rule of law in Canada by submitting the legislation, if adopted, to the courts instead. That task, in good conscience, should not fall to us.

5. Canadian Territorial Rights

Separation from Canada entails Partition of Quebec

Should, at some future time, the government secure a majority substantial enough to provoke negotiations on separation with the rest of the country, government leaders should be aware that before, during, and after the course of those negotiations, loyal Canadians resident in Quebec *will* assert their right to remain politically and territorially part of Canada. In short, separation will entail the partition of Quebec. We must recall Quebec has no right to secede under international law. The perilous course plotted by the *Draft Bill on the Sovereignty of Quebec* — legislative rebellion, a unilateral declaration of independence requiring international recognition for legitimacy — is doomed to failure. The only approach left open to the government of Quebec is the approach of René Lévesque — negotiated break-up, during the process of which, to cite McGill constitutional expert Stephen Scott:

> The Canadian federation [will be] fully entitled, *if* it is prepared to grant independence to Quebec, to impose what terms and conditions it pleases, more particularly as to territory.... The people of Canada have the sovereign right to say 'yes' or to say 'no' to the dismemberment of Canada; or to say 'yes,' but on conditions which they consider proper.

The assertion of the *Draft Bill on the Sovereignty of Quebec* that "Quebec shall retain the boundaries it has within the Canadian Confederation at the time section 1 comes into force" is therefore false and cannot be enforced.

If Canada is divisible, then Quebec is divisible

No matter what principle is used to justify Quebec's separation from Canada, the same principle can be used to justify the rights of Canadians in Quebec to remain Canadian. If, as premier Parizeau has recently stated in the Assembly, the prime reason for separation is ethnic hostility within Canada, that is to say because Quebecers "cannot be the allies of Canadians if we are both like two scorpions in a bottle," because "Canada ... is becoming psychologically unbearable to both communities" in this most decentralized of federations, then there is every reason to assume that the ethnic Quebec state proposed by separatists, a *unitary* state with no particular autonomy provided to its constituent parts, will bring those same psychological pressures *inside* Quebec to the cracking point. On the other hand, if as the leader of Canada's Official Opposition, Lucien Bouchard, has stated, the nationalism of Quebec is territorial, not ethnic, then that same territorial nationalism can apply to those areas of Quebec that wish to remain politically part of

Canada. And if the paramount principle involved in this dispute is the people's consent to be governed, then once again those within the territory of Quebec who wished to be governed by the institutions and values of their Canadian heritage should be free so to choose, and should legitimately expect the protection and encouragement of their federal government in that choice. As the authors of the *Final Report of the York University Constitutional Reform Project* noted:

> ... Where a majority of the citizens of Quebec no longer wish to remain citizens of Canada, there should be good-faith negotiations designed to achieve separation in a manner that respects the rights and interests of all involved.

> At the same time, it is evident that this democratic rationale only applies with respect to those citizens who do, in fact, wish to secede from Canada. Where there are discrete and readily identifiable blocks of persons who are geographically contiguous to the rest of Canada, a different set of considerations would seem to apply.

> It can be argued that these Canadian citizens ought not to be compelled to become citizens of an independent Quebec against their will.... The same logic which supports Quebec secession in the first place suggests that every reasonable effort should be made to give effect to the desires of those citizens who wish to remain within Canada.

Former premier of Saskatchewan, Allan Blakeney, himself an expert in constitutional law, agrees:

> If we have learned anything in this post World War II era about creating new nations, it is that, subject to pressing geographic realities, we should do every-

thing we can to ensure that all the people who want to be part of the new state be included, and all those who don't, be excluded, leaving as few minority pockets as possible. Any other course is to invite continuing difficulties arising from unhappy minorities. The list of failures of nations sought to be created upon pre-partition boundaries is long and growing, Cyprus, Ireland, Armenia, several countries in Africa, now, as it appears, the republics of Yugoslavia. Let us not add Canada/Quebec to the list.

In short, as former prime minister Pierre Elliot Trudeau long ago suggested, if Canada is divisible, then Quebec is divisible; if Quebec is indivisible, so too is Canada. Kenneth McNaught, professor emeritus of history at the University of Toronto and editor of *The Penguin History of Canada* recently wrote:

> Equality of rights in a constitutional democracy requires the full application of democracy — not a resort to unconstitutional methods. ...We must provide the constitutional means by which *every* person living in [Quebec] can decide whether to remain Canadian or join an ethnically defined republic.

> ... Mr. Parizeau convinces no one when he blusters about Quebec leaving Canada with its present provincial territory intact. Northern Quebec (Ungava), comprising well over half the province's territory, was allotted to Quebec *as a province of Canada* by Canadian legislation; it is also subject to very strong aboriginal claims which Ottawa has a fiduciary responsibility to safeguard.

> Other claims, legal and historical, would also be asserted — by aboriginals and people living in "West Quebec" and the Eastern Townships. Application of democratic self-determination for *all* the people of the province is the only way to avoid the rocks of legal-historical acrimony.

*D*espite the warnings of the Equality Party and others, later echoed in Patrick Monahan's excellent *C.D. Howe Institute Study,* Coming to Terms with Plan B [January '95], *many Canadian commentators continued to wax equivocal about the legalities of Jacques Parizeau's UDI intentions. Was the* Draft Bill on the Sovereignty of Quebec *legal? Could the PQ get away with it? In the absence of the federal government referring the entire question to the courts, Canadians could be forgiven for their uncertainties. In December of 1994 the* Special Committee for Canadian Unity *requested that Prime Minister Jean Chrétien seek the opinion of the Supreme Court on the matter, before the referendum expected that fall. In February 1995 Prime Minister Chrétien refused. During a Westmount-St. Henri by-election that month, former Bourassist Lucienne Robillard secured the approval of the* Bloc Québécois *candidate when she said she would not challenge the legality of the PQ's Draft Bill and nor would the federal government. Paul Wells'* Gazette *piece,* "It would be legal if it works" *was typical of the prevailing confusion, one that dominated the '95 referendum debate and which, we now know, saw Canada come perilously close to the chaos of a UDI Parizeau was prepared to issue within days of a YES victory.*

Special Committee Letter to the Prime Minister

via the offices of Pearl & Associates
December 9, 1994

Dear Prime Minister:

Our firm has been engaged to act on behalf of the *Special Committee for Canadian Unity,* a group of concerned responsible citizens in Quebec who believe that the future of our nation lies in maintaining a unified country under a federal system of government.

As you are aware, the premier of Quebec, Mr. Jacques Parizeau, has, on December 6th, 1994, tabled before the National Assembly of Quebec, a draft bill entitled *An Act respecting the sovereignty of Quebec.* This proposed Act will (once passed and assented to) purport to declare the Province of Quebec to be a sovereign country, with effect one year (or earlier if the National Assembly so orders) after approval is given in a referendum by the voters of the Province of Quebec.

Regardless of the ultimate outcome of a referendum, such an Act is bound to have an immediate, and serious, destablilizing effect on the country as a whole. Even the presentation of the draft bill is a matter of grave concern. Interest rates, levels of economic activity, and even the health of financial institutions are all affected, and will be more affected when the bill is passed and receives Royal assent.

It is therefore of great importance to contest the validity of this proposed Act before the courts of law as promptly as possible. Ordinary litigants are (on the prevailing legal consensus) not entitled to institute legal proceedings prior to Royal assent being given to this bill, which would not occur until late March 1995. The government of your province, however, has immediate access to the Supreme Court of Canada.

With respect, it would therefore seem appropriate, and in the public interest of the entire country, that your government immediately submit a reference to the Supreme Court of Canada:

> Is it within the legislative authority of a province of Canada, under the Constitution of Canada, to enact a statute declaring that province to be a sovereign state, and if such a statute is enacted, what is its force and effect?

We note in particular sub-section 52(1) of the *Constitution Act, 1982,* which states:

> (1) The Constitution of Canada is the supreme law of Canada, and any law that is inconsistent with the provisions of the Constitution, is, to the extent of the inconsistency, of no force or effect.

We note also sub-section 52(3) which provides:

(3) Amendments to the Constitution of Canada shall
    be made only in accordance with the authority
    contained in the Constitution of Canada.

The relevant provisions conferring powers of constitutional amendment are to be found in Part V of the 1982 Act, entitled "Procedure for Amending Constitution of Canada." Read with the other provisions of Part V, and with s. 52, s. 45 empowers a provincial legislature *only* to alter the *internal* provincial constitution, and even this is subject to restrictions. The textual provisions are clear, and the judicial authorities are ample. The draft Bill, by contrast, attempts to throw an aura of normalcy, legitimacy, and even specious legality, over a revolutionary action, the overthrow of the Canadian state.

We are therefore urging you, as the Prime Minister of Canada, immediately to submit the above question as to whether or not it is open to the legislature of a Canadian province, by its own act, to declare the province to be a sovereign country. This, of course, is the substance of the proposed Quebec statute as expressed in section 1, which provides: "Quebec is a sovereign country."

We would be pleased to consult with you, if you wish, with respect to any matters that may be relevant to the foregoing. We enclose, for your information, a copy of the draft Bill.

❖

Response of the Prime Minister of Canada to the Special Committee

February 7, 1995

Messieurs:

This is further to your letter of December 9, 1994, regarding the draft Bill called *An Act respecting the Sovereignty of Quebec* tabled by the Quebec Government in the National Assembly on December 6, 1994.

In your letter, you request that the Government submit a reference to the Supreme Court of Canada asking whether it is within the legislative authority of a province, under the Constitution of Canada, to enact a statute declaring that province to be a sovereign state, and if such a statute is enacted, what is its force or effect.

I am of the view that the central issue in the months ahead is whether or not the citizens of Quebec want to stay in Canada, and that we should not allow ourselves to be side-tracked into a discussion of how separation might occur. I strongly believe the best way to deal with the separatists is to make sure they carry the burden of proof to show why separating from Canada would be in the best interests of Quebecers. Therefore, although I understand the reasons why the *Committee for Canadian Unity* wishes to see the legality of the draft bill questioned, I do not agree that, in the present circumstances, the course you are recommending would be an advisable one for the Government of Canada.

Thank you for bringing your suggestion to my attention and that of the Premiers.

It Would Be Legal If It Works: Experts

by Paul Wells:
reprinted from the Gazette
March 27, 1995

When federal Justice Minister Allan Rock said last December [1994] that the Quebec government's draft bill on sovereignty was unconstitutional, Quebec sovereignists accused him of interfering. But Rock also got in trouble with some Canadian federalists for declaring, almost in the same breath, that the constitutionality of separation was a mere "technical detail" compared to the will of Quebecers to decide their own future.

It was an uncomfortable moment for Rock, but such are the wages of daring to wade into the Quebec sovereignty debate. The paradox is that many constitutional experts agree that Rock was right when he said, essentially, that Quebec can't go, but Canada can't stop it. Or, to state the paradox more precisely, if Quebec attempts to secede without Canada's co-operation, it will find nothing in Canadian law — and precious little in international law — to support the move. But law alone will have little bearing on the success of secession. As *Université Laval* professor Henri Brun puts it, the test of Quebec's right to separate is "whether it works." Welcome to the complex, and seemingly contradictory, debate over whether Quebec could pull off a "unilateral declaration of independence" (UDI) — an attempt to become a new country without the legal sanction of the country it's currently part of, Canada.

It's not just a theoretical debate, because premier Jacques Parizeau's draft bill on sovereignty is a recipe for a UDI. It says Quebec would become "a sovereign country" a year after the bill's approval by a majority in a referendum. It also provides for negotiations during that year. The endlessly complex talks — involving Quebec, Ottawa, and perhaps other provinces — could conceivably produce, within a year, an agreement on a formal amendment to the Canadian constitution, letting Quebec out. But the one year sovereignty deadline would not be conditional on the outcome of the negotiations. Deal or no deal, Quebec would be out the door.

This makes Referendum '95 an altogether different affair from the *Parti Québécois's* last rendezvous with destiny, in 1980. Fifteen years ago then-premier René Lévesque was seeking only a "mandate to negotiate" political separation from, and economic links with, Canada. As Osgoode Hall law professor Patrick Monahan has written, "far from asserting that Quebec could secede unilaterally, the (1980) referendum was premised on the assumption that secession was a matter of negotiation with the rest of Canada." This time, Parizeau is taking every opportunity to emphasize that — while he welcomes and expects negotiations with Canada about several matters — the sovereignty of Quebec is not to be haggled over.

Parizeau understands that with a UDI, Quebec would, in the words of University of Western Ontario professor Robert Young, "step outside the existing constitutional order." Last December, when Rock and Prime Minister Jean Chrétien were telling interviewers Parizeau's draft bill didn't obey the constitution, Parizeau's reaction was as telling as it was contemptuous. "Well, they're discovering that a little late. The legitimacy that these people in Ottawa are questioning is drawn from the people itself. It is the Quebec people that will decide," Parizeau went on. "It is the Quebec people, by virtue of their own laws, which will decide their own future."

To which a reasonable observer might respond: Hey, can he do that? Maybe. Let's look at what Canadian law has to say about Quebec secession, and then at international law. Finally, we'll consider how much influence laws of any kind can have over the outcome of events.

UDIs are nothing new. The term came into the lexicon on Nov. 11, 1966, when Ian Smith declared Rhodesia's independence from British colonial rule and installed a whites-only government in that overwhelmingly black African country (now black-ruled and known as Zimbabwe.) Several former Soviet republics declared their independence from the Soviet Union at the beginning of the '90s, some with overwhelming support in referendums, some without even bothering to hold referendums. Not all secessions have been preceded by UDIs, however, Austria and Hungary separated by mutual accord in 1867. In 1992 the Czech and Slovak republics were created by an act of the Czechoslovak federal government, after the Slovaks had threatened to secede unilaterally. But it's not clear what lessons any of these events have for Canada. Rhodesia's secession was a version of decolonialization. Austria-Hungary and Czechoslovakia were looser federations than Canada. As Young has written, "there has never been a case of secession in an advanced, capitalist, democratic country." Quebec would be the first.

Neither of Canada's main constitutional documents, the *Constitution Acts* of 1867 and 1982 contains provisions for the departure of any province or territory from confederation. It might be tempting to say that's enough to close the debate: separation isn't in the constitution, so it's unconstitutional, so it can't happen. This sort of reasoning would bring airplanes crashing to the ground the moment they stray into Canadian airspace, because the constitution is mute about air travel, too. The real utility of a constitution is in adapting to new situations. Even if the constitution doesn't fit a new situation, it can be made to do so by amending the constitution.

Several scholars have suggested Canada's constitution could be amended to allow for Quebec to secede constitutionally. In effect, the parts that mention Quebec would be deleted, and other parts such as those dealing with the distribution of seats in the Parliament, would be modified to reflect a smaller, reshaped Canada. These changes would take the approval of the House of Commons, the Senate, and the legislatures of at least seven provinces, seven which have half of Canada's population. Osgoode's Patrick Monahan argues that Quebec secession would require other amendments — to the offices of governor-general and lieutenant governor, for instance — that need unanimous approval of all provincial legislatures to pass. And because the constitution gives Ottawa responsibility over native populations that would be affected by Quebec secession, Monahan thinks native groups would also have to be at the bargaining table.

This is all starting to look a lot like the negotiations that led to the doomed Meech and Charlottetown Accords. There is no guarantee that a workable set of amendments could get unanimous agreement — especially since no government outside Quebec has a mandate from its voters to discuss such weighty matters. Hence the temptation not even to bother trying. With a UDI, a separatist government attempts to set up a new legal regime on its territory, to replace the old set of laws. "This is a very serious act," Western's Young writes. Indeed, it fits the strict legal definition of a revolutionary act.

"Whether this kind of legal revolution occurs," Monahan writes, "depends ultimately on whether the new regime can successfully oust the old one." This can happen with little conflict if Canada simply accepts the UDI and recognizes Quebec sovereignty. Or it can happen with more conflict if Canada rejects the UDI and competes with the Quebec government to see whose legal regime can prevail on Quebec soil. The result of a contested UDI is "a contest of national will, possibly through forceful means," Young writes. At one end of that conflict is

a series of tedious legal battles between governments. At the other end, at least in theory, is civil
war (which just about nobody predicts for Quebec.)
It is impossible to predict, Young writes, where on
this spectrum we would end up.

What does international law say about Quebec's right to secede unilaterally? Nothing conclu-
sive. Historian Desmond Morton has described the
international attitude to secession as "political ex-
pediency flavoured by opportune moral outrage."
Historically, the world has welcomed secessions that
worked and condemned those that didn't. Those
who support a UDI generally make a three part argument — that Quebecers constitute a people; that
the Quebec people have a right to self-determination; and that that right includes a right to secede.
As Young points out, there's room to argue about
each of those points.

What defines a people? Most obvious answers
— language, race, religion — clearly don't apply to
the entire Quebec population. Or they describe
groups that spill across Quebec's borders, such as
francophone Canadians. Daniel Turp, the *Bloc Québécois's* constitutional adviser has suggested Quebecers define themselves through a *"vouloir vivre
collectif,"* a collective will to exist. But how is that
will expressed? In a referendum vote? In that case,
the people who vote against the majority have ap-
parently opted out of the collective will, and it's hard
to count them as part of the Quebec people.

Still, let's assume Quebecers constitute a people, and move on to Quebec's right to self-determination. Some observers have argued that only peo-

ples experiencing foreign oppression, or living in racist regimes that deny them rights enjoyed by other, have a right to self-determination. This is the opinion of five international legal experts hired by the Bélanger-Campeau Commission in 1991 to study Quebec's right to secede. Parizeau often quotes other parts of this "five experts" opinion, but he never mentions this part of their argument.

Canadian politicians have, though, often acknowledged Quebec's right to self-determination. Progressive Conservatives, for instance, overwhelmingly endorsed that right at a 1991 policy convention. But does that right go so far as to include the right to secede without Canada's legal sanction?

The touchstone here is the none too succinctly named 1970 *Declaration of Principles of International Law concerning Friendly Relations and Co-operation among States in Accordance with the Charter of the United Nations*. This document says self-determination doesn't include the right to "dismember or impair ... sovereign and independent states conducting themselves in compliance with the principle of equal rights and self-determination of peoples." In sum, international law gives Quebec the right to secede if Quebecers are oppressed. This gives rise to some fascinating arguments. The *Bloc's* Turp, for instance, has suggested that if Canada doesn't co-operate with Quebec's attempt to secede, Quebecers would thus become oppressed — and therefore have the right to secede. Who said constitutional law was no fun?

We could debate these points for the next 20 years, just as the experts have debated them for the last 20. The point, Young argues, is that "the legal issues are fundamentally contestable." In that case, the success of secession comes down to two tests: recognition of the new régime by other countries, and its ability to exert legal control throughout its territory. And foreign recognition often hinges on demonstrated control of the territory. So Quebec's secession would be endorsed by international law *if* other countries began to believe the Quebec government could adequately govern itself. "The test of Quebec's ability to become sovereign is whether it works," *Université Laval* professor Henri Brun says.

In legal control, as in international recognition, the key "foreign" player would be Canada. Canada might contest Quebec's secession. José Woehrling, a *Université de Montréal* law professor who supports sovereignty, expects that the federal government would reject the use of armed force but use an array of other methods: "organization of a pan Canadian referendum to consult the population of the other provinces on the departure of Quebec; systematic court challenges of all acts passed by the secessionist government; enactment of the Emergency Measures Act and suspension of civil liberties ...."

As long as this contest between governments continued, other countries would hesitate to recognize Quebec sovereignty, for fear of taking sides in what Canada would regard as an internal matter. Parizeau's foreign trips to seek international recognition of a sovereign Quebec are meaningless, Monahan argues, because any conflict would be over before other countries' recognition would be relevant. "It is all well and good for (French presidential candidate Jacques) Chirac to say, 'We would recognize

Quebec if it becomes independent,'" Monahan says. "But becoming independent involves a lot more than a few politicians standing up on TV and saying, 'We think we're independent.'"

Would Canada try to block Quebec's unilateral secession? Again, nobody agrees. As University of British Columbia professor Alan Cairns has pointed out, it's not even clear what 'Canada' would be in this case. The federal government, led by a Quebecer? A special parliamentary committee with *Bloc* representatives? A Meech-minus-one collection of provincial premiers and aboriginal leaders? *(See Who Could Speak for Rest of Canada, p. A8.)* Beyond that, would Canada's interest lie in stretching out the confrontation, prolonging the devastating effects of uncertainty on both sides? Or in cutting a deal as soon as possible?

Here are two possible futures: Monahan says a UDI, since it would include no guarantee from Quebec about sharing Canada's huge debt, would be unacceptable to Canada. Ottawa would be forced into "a high-stakes game of constitutional chicken" with Quebec, until the flight of international investment capital from both sides forces one side to give in. Quebec would stay in Canada, broken and, for once, truly humiliated. Or Canada, bled dry and on the verge of shattering, would let Quebec go.

Young expects it would never get to a UDI. Immediately after a majority vote for sovereignty, he says, Canada's government would be forced into negotiating Quebec's secession. The negotiations would go rapidly, impose severe short term costs on both sides, but allow a viable sovereign Quebec and a viable rest-of-Canada to emerge from the crisis.

Why would Ottawa bargain, and why would (rest of) Canadians let it? To avoid the bottomless uncertainty of a confrontation, Young says. Until Quebec's future became settled, nobody in Canada could be sure of the value of their bank deposits, pensions, passports, stocks, contracts, even train tickets. Their legal rights would be in question — which police forces would they obey? Companies wouldn't know whether trade deals guaranteeing their foreign markets would survive. "This is uncertainty," Young writes. "People will pay a lot to avoid it.... This price includes not only economic losses but also political costs — the distaste of having matters handled by a government that one did not support, the frustration of having decisions made without participating in them, and the irritation of one's leaders making deals with separatists."

It's Not Legal

by Keith Henderson:
reprinted from the Gazette
March 27, 1995

P aul Wells' equivocal piece "It would be legal if it works: experts" suggests the legal issues surrounding Quebec's secession are just too confusing, uncertain, and unresolvable to provide Canadians with much comfort in the lead-up to the coming referendum. Wells is wrong.

First, nothing is legal "if it works." That is like declaring robbery 'legal' if you can get away with it. Things become legal if they are assented to by due process, and under the rule of law, that includes the exercise of political authority. Power is not a purse-snatching. In a democracy, the right to govern is ringed round with elaborate rules of consent by those governed and with the checks and balances of the rights of neighbours. The proposition, "It's legal if it works" is nothing more than street-gang politics writ large.

Nor does the constitution of Canada have to specify secession as expressly illegal in order to make it so, as Wells implies. The BNA Act outlines the powers a provincial government may exercise. No provincial government in Canada may simply arrogate to itself *all* powers — i.e. conduct a referendum, win it, and declare itself sovereign — and remain legally within the bounds of the constitution. Wells' answer to his own question, "Hey, can he do that?" — "Maybe" — is false. Parizeau cannot, and the very fact that most scholars agree constitutional amendment would be necessary to enable Parizeau 'to do that' is proof enough. Thank god, there are far more legal certainties in Canada than Wells' calculated ambiguities suggest.

Wells then attempts to undermine the testimony of the five international experts before the Bélanger-Campeau Commission by stating that "international law gives Quebec the right to secede if Quebecers are oppressed." International law gives no such thing. In fact, the five experts were quite categorical about this. "The Quebec people effectively exercises its right to self-determination within the framework of the Canadian whole and is not legally well founded to invoke it to justify a future accession to independence," they said. "The right to secession does not exist in international law."

Finally, Wells asks, "Would Canada try to block Quebec's unilateral secession?" and concludes "Again, nobody agrees." Again, Wells is wrong. As proof, he cites Osgoode Hall constitutional expert Patrick Monahan who says Canada *would* contest a UDI and whom Wells (utterly unfairly) characterizes as someone who would "stretch out confrontation" and "prolong devastating economic uncertainty" and whose option, if successful, would keep Quebec in Canada, "broken and, for once, truly humiliated." What Wells ignores here, of course, is that with a 51-52% majority, it would be separatists doing these humiliating, not to mention suicidally adventurous things to Quebec and to Canada — in the name of less than 10% of the population of the country — not Canadians who happen to agree with Patrick Monahan.

Far more approvingly, Wells cites Robert Young, who favours quick acquiescence to separatists' demands and whom Wells quotes as expecting "it will never get to a UDI." (If this is true, Robert Young hasn't read Parizeau's *Draft Bill* which *is* a UDI.) From Young's painless separation perspective, all proceeds smoothly and expeditiously with the federal government ceding whenever needed. What Wells doesn't mention, of course, is that at a recent meeting of Canadian intellectuals sponsored by the C.D. Howe Institute, Young was the *only* invitee who argued this way, his position very much in the minority, all others taking Monahan's much stronger line. Paul Wells says nobody agrees, but the shape of a much firmer consensus in Canada is emerging, including solid federalists like Stéphane Dion and Marcel Coté, all of whom, like the Equality Party, give far more credence to the legal arguments against secession than it would seem, does the *Gazette.*

*G*uy Bertrand and I first crossed paths in February
'95 at a McGill University conference where Bertrand echoed some of the arguments Equality had long
been making about the tax chaos Canada would face after
a UDI. Bertrand subsequently pressed the legal case
against the Parizeau Draft Bill, in tandem with Stephen
Scott, and won a major September '95 pre-referendum
victory before Superior Court Justice Robert Lesage. The
Lesage decision, while it refused to grant Bertrand's request to shut down the referendum itself, stated that the
Parizeau Bill constituted "a serious threat to the rights
and freedoms of the plaintiff granted by the Canadian
Charter of Rights and Freedoms" and "a repudiation
of the Constitution of Canada." The moral bankruptcy of
the Referendum NO Committee under Quebec Liberal
leader Daniel Johnson and key federal Liberals and Conservatives became clear when the NO leadership refused
to make Bertrand's victory part of the NO campaign,
marginalized its significance, and prevented others from
raising the issue themselves. Bertrand spoke once with
Equality Party and other Special Committee leaders on
October 26, 1995, during the one referendum event we
were entitled to hold, where all participants raised the
significance of the legal issues and the possibility of partition in the event of a YES. No media, either English or
French, bothered to cover the meeting. Bertrand's book,
Plaidoyer pour les Citoyens, *appeared in May '96.*

Guy Bertrand's *Plaidoyer pour les Citoyens*

by Keith Henderson:
reprinted from The Financial Post
June 24, 1996

Sometimes it's the small, human things in a book that attract, no less so in Guy Bertrand's political testament, *Plaidoyer pours les Citoyens*. Bertrand is the Quebec City lawyer, founding member of the PQ, whose 180 degree turn toward Canada two years ago earned him justified praise in some federalist circles, suspicion in others, and the contempt of his former separatist allies. One of those touching moments in the book is when Bertrand admits that his political convictions have cost him contact with his brother Rosaire, an advisor to Lucien Bouchard. Bertrand now leaves his brother telephone messages, this despite his mother's deathbed wish that her sons would never abandon one another. Darker still is the story Bertrand tells of meeting a Quebec judge, a former separatist comrade, who refused to shake his hand. When Bertrand answered good-humouredly that everyone was entitled to his own opinions in a democracy, the judge responded: "You're not only a traitor, you deserve the worst fate one can reserve for them."

Brother breaking with brother over politics — it was there 50 years ago in MacLennan's *Two Solitudes.* Paul Tallard felt a total stranger in his brother Marius' house, because Marius took the side of Quebec's priests who had "turned the whole Church into a nationalist political party." Guy Bertrand sees the same problem in 1996. "Sad to say, fanatical egocentric nationalism has at its heart the same divisive seeds we used to find forty years ago in Quebec, whenever questions of religion were raised.... We didn't accept that a catholic became a Protestant or converted to another religion. It was considered treason. In the *Parti Québécois,* it's 'believe or die.' Those who refuse the dogma aren't worth knowing and can't form part of the family; they're traitors."

Fortunately for the Canadian-minded among us, Bertrand extends his iconoclasm even further. He's one federalist who doesn't choke on the words *status quo,* not in his view, a synonym for stagnation, but an opportunity for a more efficient sharing of powers between federal and provincial governments. Nor does Bertrand think it necessary to constitutionalize Quebec's status as a 'distinct society' since most Canadians already recognize that fact. "Quebec is legally and constitutionally equal to the other provinces and the other provinces are equal to it," he writes, including Prince Edward Island, because "the scope of a society is not measured by the extent of its territory or the number of its inhabitants, but by the dignity, heart, intelligence, and good will of those who live there.... All the citizens of Canada are equal, regardless of their origin." One could only wish his iconoclasm extended to Bill 101, for which Bertrand, it seems, still harbours vestiges of nationalist affinity.

However, the heart of the book is Bertrand's legal case against separatist plans to secede unilaterally from Canada. It is a case for which Canadians owe Guy Bertrand an immense debt of gratitude, because by undertaking it, at his own expense, he has filled a void left by a derelict federal government, asserted the constitutional authority of Canada's judiciary in an area where Quebec's provincialists have had free rein for years, and perhaps most importantly, clarified the terms of the debate. How often have we heard from nationalist choristers, including Daniel Johnson, that 50% + 1 was *the* rule of democracy and that Quebec could secede at will after conducting whatever Quebec-only referendum on the subject it chose? The Bertrand case makes clear that the National Assembly cannot be used to destroy Canada's constitution. Secession can only occur on the basis of constitutional amendment, i.e. with Canadian consent. Referendums can occur, but they are purely consultative.

Here *Plaidoyer pour les Citoyens* has raised some instructive historical parallels. In 1867 the Nova Scotia legislature tried to secede unilaterally from Canada based on a petition signed by 80% of the population. The privy council struck down the legislation on the grounds that Nova Scotia had not secured the agreement of the other 3 provinces. In the 1860s Texas tried much the same thing. A Guy Bertrand of the day took the matter to the US Supreme Court which ruled as follows: "The union between Texas and the other States was as complete and perpetual, and as indissoluble as the Union between the original States. There was no place for reconsideration, or revocation, except through revolution, or through consent of the States." In 1938 Western Australia conducted a referendum and issued a UDI. The Australian constitution required a pan-Australia referendum to permit secession, and Australians rejected this idea. Today Western Australia remains part of the federation and Australia now has an indivisibility clause in its constitution.

Bertrand, to this Canadian's delight, has now taken his case one step further. He wants the Quebec Superior Court to declare *ultra vires* any use of Quebec's referendum law to sanction a unilateral declaration of independence. One can only wish him god speed.

*E*quality spent the summer of '95 preparing its case for participating in the expected fall referendum. In Quebec that meant asking the head of the Quebec Liberal Party, Daniel Johnson, putative leader of the NO campaign, for permission to form, along with our allies in the Special Committee for Canadian Unity, *what under the Quebec Referendum Act is called an 'affiliated group.' The concept of an 'affiliated group' was introduced into the law before the 1980 referendum to allow people who favoured the YES or the NO, but for reasons different from the main committees, to organize and spend money legally. Equality wanted to raise three issues during the '95 campaign, the same ones we raised during the '94 election — that 50% + 1 in a Quebec-only referendum was not sufficient to begin negotiating the break-up of Canada, that the Parizeau* Draft Bill on the Sovereignty of Quebec *was illegal and unconstitutional, and that if Canada was divisible, so was Quebec, i.e. the price of Quebec's independence would be the partition of the province. The answer of the executive committee of the NO, made up of representatives of the Quebec Liberal Party, the federal Liberal Party, and the federal Conservatives, was simple — NO. Equality was forced to go to court to defend its right to free speech during a campaign on the future of the country, a campaign which Daniel Johnson's weakness and equivocations nearly lost. The irony is that Equality's arguments, suppressed by federal and provincial Liberals alike in 1995, now form the basis of Ottawa's increasingly successful 'Plan B' initiative against separatists' intended Referendum III.*

Quebec's Draconian Referendum Act

by Keith Henderson:
reprinted from The Financial Post
August 23, 1996

S ome Canadians are fond of calling October 30, 1995 Canada's near-death experience. According to them, had a small-sized football stadium of people gone YES rather than NO that night, Quebecers would have woken up the next morning in a new state. A foolish view perhaps, but wide-spread, a sure sign of Canadians' ignorance of their own law and the place of referendums in their country. Referendums in Canada are purely consultative, glorified and expensive opinion polls. They don't substitute for parliament. They neither create nor undo law. Despite what our separatist friends pretend, they don't legally underpin unilateral declarations of independence.

That doesn't mean we shouldn't take them seriously or worry about how they're conducted. It's surprising those who feel Canada lives and dies by referendum have paid so little attention to Quebec's referendum law, one of the most draconian in the western world and certainly one of the most anti-

Canadian pieces of legislation the PQ ever enacted. Yet successive federal governments have agreed to roll the dice on the country under its appalling terms without a whimper of protest. For 9 years a Liberal government, more federaloid than federalist, controlled the National Assembly and never once proposed a serious amendment. So with Liberal complicity Canada has become the only G7 nation (and the only advanced democracy) where secessionist forces are free to devise separatist referendum questions, supervise the ballot, prevent other citizens from participating, and threaten to jump outside the law based on a favourable result. The Quebec legislature rewards such bizarre practices with near unanimous approval.

Canadians could welcome a few changes here. Why should Quebec governments be entitled to conceal the fact that the referendum proposals they float before the public might, if implemented, be illegal and unconstitutional? Shouldn't people know this before they're asked to vote? All referendum questions should be fast-tracked to the courts to determine whether or not acting on an affirmative vote would violate the constitution or impact on federal law. If the courts say that's the case, Ottawa should approve the question, help conduct the ballot, and participate in the process according to federal, not provincial law.

Why should all citizens be forced to line up behind either the Quebec premier or the Leader of the Opposition and get their approval to say anything or spend a cent? There may be a YES and a NO, but there aren't just two ways to argue for them. Other parties and citizens groups should have the

automatic right to form committees affiliated to either option, to marshal their arguments, and to
spend money. That's not the way it worked last fall.
While Lucien Bouchard lied, tugged at heart strings,
and waved magic wands, Liberals ran their campaign almost exclusively on economics. Those who
wished to discuss the real consequences of illegal
separation — breaking the terms of Canada's constitution, division of debt, borders, the rights of Canadians to stay Canadian in the areas where they
form the majority — were denied status by the two
Liberal parties running the umbrella NO committee, which forced them to spend three weeks of a
four week campaign in court, trying to get approval
to spend money legally and speak their minds. When
the courts ruled their rights to freedom of speech
had indeed been violated, Liberals proceeded to use
their power under the law to set spending limits for
affiliated groups.

What, in their wisdom, did the NO mavens (including Jean Charest) think discussing the Constitution of Canada was worth? $2500. Under the same
referendum law, individuals are legally entitled to
donate up to a maximum of $3000 for the option of
their choice. The effect of the NO decision was to
say that no single individual in Quebec could exercise his rights to earmark $3000 and have the consti-
tution of Canada raised during a debate on the future of his country.

Nor are these concerns merely academic. If
Lucien Bouchard calls another referendum, it will
be fought under the same law, subject to the same
unreasonable interpretations. Once again those who
wish to raise questions of territory, debt, constitu-

tional legality, and the primacy of the rule of law will find themselves shut up, their coffers locked, and their message consigned to the margins. Canadians can't afford a recurrence of what happened on October 30. For their own future — and their children's — Quebec's Referendum Act must be changed.

*T*hrough the efforts of lawyers Brent Tyler and Guy Bertrand, Equality and the Special Committee for Canadian Unity *defeated the NO committee in court. A judicial tribunal ruled that the NO committee had violated our rights to freedom of speech. Despite that victory, for 3 weeks out of 4, no one in Quebec heard of the illegality of the YES side proposals or of their territorial implications for the province — partition — should the YES win. That was because, until the case was heard, the* Special Committee *couldn't legally spend a cent or hold a meeting to advance our arguments. And when the Committee was vindicated, Liberals turned around and used spending limit provisions of the law effectively to muzzle our arguments all over again. The results spurred Equality to take three steps. To begin with, we devised the first comprehensive set of amendments to the* Quebec Referendum Act *ever proposed. Secondly, we appealed the $2500 spending limit in court because we considered it an effective extension of the NO Committee's initial violation of our freedom of speech, a case still pending. Thirdly, we took action for damages against all members of the NO Committee for violating our rights to freedom of expression in the first place.*

Quebec Referendum Legislation:

Principles & Proposals for Reform

1. General principle — Freedom of expression

The Equality Party rejects the existing *Referendum Act* rules which require that participation in the referendum process take place exclusively through two official (so-called 'national') committees established in favour, respectively, of two positions, YES and NO. The Act now effectively denies to third persons the freedom to express and promote their views on issues of legitimate public interest and concern. It assumes that there can be only two points of view on any matter, however complex.

In seeking to give rights to two *options,* it denies both freedom and equality to *citizens.* The existing Act forces all ideas into two artificially-defined compartments. It drastically rations citizens' rights to engage in activities of free expression normal in any free society, such as printing books, newspapers, magazines or pamphlets; leasing premises for meetings; and advertising on radio and television. Persons who seek no public financing should be free to express their views at their own expense by any means they wish.

Assuming, however, that the present general scheme will be maintained, the Equality Party proposes various reforms to mitigate the inequities and abuses of the existing legislation. These proposals, however, are made without prejudice to the party's general position stated above.

2. Referenda should be consultative only

Referenda held under any provincial referendum legislation should be consultative and advisory only. The Equality Party proposes abolition of the "triggering" mechanism of section 7(b) of the *Referendum Act,* which causes bills previously passed by the National Assembly and approved by the electors in a referendum to be presented for royal assent and become law without further deliberation in the House.

3. Prior judicial determination of jurisdiction

Where a referendum question concerns a legislative proposal, the referendum should not take place until it has been finally determined by the Courts whether or not the enactment and implementation of that proposal would exceed the jurisdiction of the provincial legislature, or would, for any other reason (including inconsistency with federal laws or infringement of constitutional guarantees) involve any breach of the constitution of Canada.

4. Conditions of issuing referendum writs

Writs instituting the holding of a referendum should not be issued until all of the following conditions have been satisfied:

(i) The Courts have determined either that the legislative proposal submitted to referendum would, indeed, be constitutionally lawful and valid, or, on the contrary, that the referendum proposal would require that the Constitution of Canada, or federal laws, first be amended.

(ii) Where the referendum proposal would involve any change in the Constitution or laws of Canada, agreement has been reached between the Government of Quebec and the Government of Canada both on the referendum question itself and on the basis on which the Government of Canada, and third persons, will participate in the referendum; and, moreover, agreement on the general referendum process including eligibility to vote, enumerating and voting procedures, and the counting of votes, recounting, and contestations.

(iii) There has been a final determination of the status of any group which is seeking official recognition as a participant in the referendum process, and of the extent of its rights of participation (including public financing) if they be in issue.

(iv) The National Assembly has approved the final text of the referendum question.

5. Right of members of Assembly to form affiliated groups

When, as is required by law, a member of the National Assembly is invited to register in favour of one of the two options between which the voters are to choose in a referendum, the member must, as a matter of right, be entitled, either alone or jointly with other members, to establish an affiliated group supporting one or other of those options.

6. Provisional by-laws

To the end that the referendum process not be obstructed by delay of the official Committees in adopting or organizing by-laws, the *Referendum Act* should itself establish provisional by-laws, drawn in fair and reasonable terms, to govern each of the official Committees, or provisional Committees; such by-laws to remain in force for each Committee until they are altered or replaced by either Committee's substituting other provisions for its own governance.

7. Applications for affiliated status

As soon as the provisional Committees have been established, any group may seek affiliated status by applying to either of the official Committees, the YES or the NO (addressing the application to the provisional or to the final Committee, as may be appropriate at the moment of application). Such an application shall be deemed to have been accepted unless formally refused within fifteen days. Appeals from refusal must continue to lie to the Referendum Council unless recourse is given directly to the superior Courts of law; and, in any case, a full appeal must lie from the Council to the superior Courts.

8. Freedom of expression of third persons

Third persons, whether they be individuals, associations, or corporations, who seek no public financing, must be entitled to participate freely in the referendum campaign, to express their opinions as they think fit, and to expend their own monies in so doing. It follows that regulated expenses under the *Referendum Act* should include no expenditure incurred by anyone save a 'national' (i.e., official) Committee, or an affiliated group.

9. Third persons participating in endeavours of 'national' Committees or affiliated groups

Such third persons should be deemed not to incur regulated expenses, even when they assist in, or otherwise participate in, endeavours of 'national' (i.e., official) Committees or affiliated groups, if, in doing so, those third persons expend their own funds, without reimbursement, for meals, lodging, or transportation.

A measure of how much Daniel Johnson and the Quebec Liberal Party learned — likely successors to the NO Committee leadership under Referendum III — is Johnson's testimony, under oath, in the action against him for violating Equality and the Special Committee's freedom of expression in '95. Johnson makes no apologies whatever for the conduct of the Quebec Liberal Party and repeats, as the following excerpts attest, the Quebec Liberal Party intention not to raise the vacuity of the PQ pretensions to a right to secede at will from the Canadian federation. Johnson also makes clear that, from the perspective of the Quebec Liberal Party, the territory of Canada is negotiable, but that of Quebec is indivisible. The inescapable conclusion is that, as far as Johnson's Liberals are concerned, Referendum III would be fought along exactly the same strategic lines as Referendum II.

Johnson Poised to Repeat Referendum Near Fiasco

NO Committee had "No position"
on dividing territory or UDI:
Press Communiqué, May 1997

Despite over a year of federalist ferment in Quebec, the gathering 'Staying Canadian' movement and the Chrétien Liberals' belated Supreme Court challenge to separatist assumptions, in surprising testimony under oath last week [May '97], Liberal leader Daniel Johnson admitted that during his leadership the pro-Canada NO Committee had no formal position on either the divisibility of Canada and Quebec or the legality of a Bouchard-Parizeau UDI. Moreover Johnson made no apologies for the oversight. "Legality, now... I didn't think I had any juridical arguments to highlight in public. The NO committee wasn't a big huge lawyer's office whose job was to demonstrate the legality or illegality of some hypothetical potential act.... You're asking me if I found on a political level I had any legal arguments to bring forward. Well, I tell you that's not my role. That's not my role as a federalist."

When asked by EP lawyer Brent Tyler if he had ever used the phrase 'If Canada is divisible, so is Quebec,' Johnson replied, "No... It is the mandate of the premier to defend Quebec's territorial integrity." Nowhere in his testimony did Johnson testify that it was his duty to defend Canada's territorial integrity, a kind of argument which he also dismissed as 'legalistic.' "I can't answer on that score as a lawyer, and the NO Committee wasn't a committee of legal experts," he said." That wasn't its purpose." The goal of the NO campaign was to win the hearts and minds of Quebecers with economic arguments, Johnson said. "The policy of the NO...was in documents which we published on the economy, on economic impacts, on financial impacts, on budgetary impacts. That's what we published during the referendum."

EP Leader Keith Henderson noted that by dismissing arguments about the unconstitutionality of a UDI Johnson was trivializing the rule of law and jettisoning not just Canada's constitutional tradition, but the values implicit in that constitution. "Canada's not a big common market for provinces, a Bourassa-like EEC of the north," Henderson said. "With no heart for Canada and no conviction about its value apart from the dollar sign, it's little wonder Johnson made such a mess last time round."

The EP leader also criticized the Quebec Liberals for not standing up for Canadians' rights to stay Canadian regardless of a YES vote. "It's Canadians who'll make the final decision about the map of the country, every square inch of which belongs to every one of them, including every square inch of Quebec. How can someone who apologized for saying he was a Canadian first on the grounds he was 'tired' be expected to defend that principle?"

Henderson also castigated Johnson for denying the Equality Party its right to freedom of expression during the last Referendum campaign. "They stifled us. The courts said so. What I can't understand is how Chrétien allowed the Feds to be stifled too, by agreeing to campaign on such a narrow, unfulfilling view of Canada. Why did they knuckle under to the Quebec Liberals? Why didn't they do what we did — form an affiliated committee, then run a campaign on the issues they're now raising? Not timidly and abjectly, as though they have to apologize for being. An articulate, smart, passionate, and daring campaign — what Canadians expected."

The Struggle Against UDI
Post-Referendum

*G*iven the closeness of the '95 Referendum result, to-gether with our allies in The Special Committee, Equality conceived and organized the now famous Moot Court meeting at the McGill University Law Faculty. The subject for discussion was partition and the threat of a UDI. Equality assembled the guest list, a sort of who's who of the Plan B movement, Stephen Scott, columnists William Johnson, Andrew Coyne and Diane Francis, the editors of Pierre Trudeau's Cité Libre, Max and Monique Nemni, Guy Bertrand, Céline Martin-Flynn of the Reform Party, and myself. We expected 3 to 4 hundred people. Two thousand showed up. Video monitors had to be set up in four adjoining rooms. Hundreds were turned away at the door. In Fighting for Canada, *Diane Francis summarized the Moot Court Meeting's impact:*

> The event was an undeniable triumph and made a difference. That was because Prime Minister Chrétien watched it on French television. He had been unable to sleep due to jet lag after a trip to Asia. The arguments about the rule of law and partition sank in. He called William Johnson after the rally to personally tell him so.
>
> Two days after the rally, federal Justice Minister Allan Rock for the first time in thirty years talked about violations of the law in Quebec and said his department might get involved in some of the court cases under way.
>
> Then two days after that bombshell, Chrétien's constitutional deputy, Stéphane Dion, talked about the possibility of partition, repeating the logic: "If Canada is divisible, then so is Quebec." The separatists were apoplectic and the Quebec press went into a frenzy....

Moot Court Rally Speech

by Keith Henderson:
January 21, 1996

C anadians have a right to political stability,"
Prime Minister Jean Chrétien said the night
after the October 30 referendum. Indeed they
do. But Jean Chrétien stayed silent on the subject of
precisely how the government of Canada would
ensure this stability. That silence, ladies and gentlemen, is the problem.

Even before October 30, 1995, Canadians knew
that if separatists lost, they would not simply go
away and leave us all alone. No, these fine demo-
crats had already announced they would never take
NO for an answer. If they lost, they'd come back
again — and again — in what has become the neu-
rotic syndrome of 'à la prochaine fois' until they either harassed or confused Quebecers into giving
them the answer they want. That is why Quebecers
must be told the full terms and conditions Canada
will lay down should ever they choose to secede.
Until Ottawa does just that, the threat of secession,
the perpetual knife to the throat of Canada, will
never be removed. People will continue to move
away; immigrants and investors will continue to
shun the province; more Quebecers will land on the

welfare rolls; Montreal, as a city, and Quebec, as a province, will deepen their poverty. Canada as a nation will suffer. Instead of finally being able to build for the future, as in any normal western democracy, we'll find ourselves, as we have in the past, constantly worrying about whether our friends and families, our heritage, and our communities will one day be wrenched from what is familiar and potentially productive and cast into what some have called a "suicidal adventure." Is it not high time for responsible people to end this perpetual game of political brinkmanship? Plain truth will do that. Not silence and indirection, ostrich politics and quisling obfuscations and evasions, but plain truth about the consequences, not just of this referendum past, but of *any* such referendum in the future — that is what will set us free from the morass of secessionist blackmail, the humiliating 'What will it take for you to stay' questions and the impossible 'Nothing, I'm a separatist' answers — the quagmire that has characterized our political processes for over a generation.

What are these plain truths I am speaking about? What should the federal government be saying now that it's not saying or doing that it's not doing? As a start, the federal government must reassure Canadians that there can be no question of a unilateral declaration of independence — UDI — by the National Assembly of Quebec. Make no mistake. Dress it as you will; call for negotiations beforehand or afterward; propose confederal joint committees or Maastrich superstructures, the *Bill on the Future of Quebec* and all other such proposals from the government of Quebec — including the one made in 1991 by the Quebec Liberal Party, Bill 150, — represent Unilateral Declarations of Independence, and as such are illegal and unconstitutional under the law of Canada. Such laws exceed the authority of provincial legislatures and therefore need not be obeyed. Such laws should never even be proposed. It is the duty of the government of Canada, as it is of all other provincial legislators and of each and every citizen of Canada, to uphold the rule of law in our country and never to submit to illegal and arbitrary measures. That is why it was not sufficient for the Prime Minister of Canada, Jean Chrétien, or for the Minister of Justice of Canada, Allan Rock, merely to declare such proposed legislation illegal and unconstitutional, as they rather timorously did with respect to the *Bill on the Future of Quebec.* The Prime Minister and Minister of Justice of Canada should have done their duty and referred such bills to the courts, whose responsibility is, as in all democracies, to pronounce on the legality of proposed legislation, particularly legislation which the people are invited to approve in a referendum. Quebecers must never again be asked to endorse illegalities — and I am certain large numbers of Quebecers would never have done so had they been made aware of the unconstitutionality of the proposals put before them. That is the first thing the federal government must see to, that no government in Canada ever again seeks popular approval for laws that cannot, democratically, be adopted.

Once it is established in everyone's mind that no province can secede from Canada without constitutional authority, i.e. that Quebec cannot become independent without Canada's consent, and that Canada will never acquiesce to a UDI, the federal government must begin laying down clearly the terms and conditions for any such secession to occur. That seems only logical. We cannot have the Prime Minister of the country, even sarcastically, inviting Quebecers to "just do it" as he did last April, without telling Canadians what 'doing it' might mean. The subject is vast, intricate, and unpleasant, but three principles strike me as vital.

First, by signalling that Canada will not acquiesce to a UDI, Ottawa will be saying to Quebec that there is no way Quebec will ever be allowed to give force and effect to illegal legislation, to impound federal taxes or to abscond from its responsibilities vis-à-vis the national debt. Jean Campeau, Jacques Parizeau and Lucien Bouchard's musings about how they will pay only the interest on Quebec's portion of the debt and not the principal must be publicly challenged and repudiated. Tampering with the Canadian armed forces by her Majesty's Disloyal Opposition must never again be tolerated and *péquiste* threats to use the police and the courts to uphold a revolutionary Quebec régime must be acknowledged by the federal government and denounced.

Secondly, by declaring that there can be no secession without Canadian consent, Ottawa will be signalling that the map of Canada will not be changed by a simple 50% + 1 vote in a Quebec-only referendum. Every square inch of this country belongs to *all* Canadians and our birthright must never be ceded or altered without all of us being consulted in a national referendum. No longer should the federal government prop up the rotten house of cards of draconian Quebec referendum law or allow separatist governments to dictate the timing, the question, the scrutineers, and the rules of the game of secession, quarantining Quebecers off from their fellow citizens or confusing them with studied ambiguities. Nor must the federal government ever again collude, as it did last October with Quebec Liberals, in the active suppression of ideas such as those you are hearing tonight, denying the freedom of expression of those who think differently and forcing them to go to court to uphold their rights to campaign as they see fit in public consultations about their future. There is more than one way to fight for Canada.

Thirdly, and more importantly, should ever a majority of Quebecers support them and separatists get their way, they cannot be permitted to assume that they'll take everyone in Quebec with them on their unsavoury adventure. Loyal Canadians in Quebec are not goods and chattels to be moved about at the whim of nationalist politicians in Quebec City. We know from polls conducted a year ago that vast numbers of loyal Canadians intend to leave the province if Quebec ever chooses independence — 59% of non-francophones and some 15% of francophones as well — an internal migration of unparalleled magnitude, some million five hundred thousand citizens, carrying with them dangerously unmanageable economic repercussions. To avoid this catastrophe, and for reasons of simple justice, loyal Canadians in Quebec must be given the assurance by their federal government that they will have the choice to remain Canadian in the territories of Quebec where they form majorities, just as the Cree up North have already been promised. In short, if Canada is divisible, then so is Quebec. The operative principle must be 'consent to be governed.' If Canadians in Quebec wish to be governed by Canada and its institutions, then so be it. Ottawa must clearly and publicly repudiate the notion that it would be necessary for loyal Canadians to move in order to retain their Canadian citizenship after a YES vote as a C.D. Howe Institute study once suggested. We must above all avoid the utter humiliation of being forced to become refugees in our own country. As a priority, if we are driven to accept secession, it is boundaries that must be moved to accommodate the principle of people's consent to be governed, not people who must be moved to accommodate boundaries. Loyal NO voters deserve no less. The Canadian government's refusal thus far to reassure its own citizens on the subject of their rights to stay Canadian, come what may, is nothing short of disgraceful.

Finally, one other remark the Prime Minister made in the wake of October 30 bears repeating. "We won," said Jean Chrétien, or words to that effect. "Twice in fifteen years the separatists have asked Quebecers to break up the country and twice we've won." Indeed, we did. But we're all aware the margin of victory was too razor-thin for us to rejoice and return to business as usual. One further step must be taken. Indebted as we are, Canadians can afford no more of these ceaseless threats to our futures. Enough is enough. Fed up with sterile separatist initiatives and the uncertainty created by so ambiguous a victory for the NO in a campaign so poorly fought because so poorly defined, I think Canadians are ready to join together to address the real issue before us and to make sure we say YES to Canada in such a way as never to put our country at risk again. One more referendum will still be required, not Bouchard's 'three-peat' on independence called at separatist whim and pleasure, not Keith Spicer's warmed over Mulroneyism, Meech Lake/Charlot-tetown revisited, the 'New Country or No Country' roll of the dice Canadians have been so disheartened by in the past. What's needed now is a victory in a pan-Canadian referendum on the indivisibility of our country. That would drive a stake through the heart of separatism, permanently remove the knife at the throat of our country, and in the process elevate Canada to the level of internal stability currently enjoyed by France, Australia, and the United States, whose constitutions already contain just such a clause. We and our children deserve nothing less.

"But Quebec will never agree to that," some of you may already be thinking. "What's the use of embarking on a sterile exercise that's doomed to failure from the start?" I say, don't be so sure. If, perhaps in the course of a *Royal Commission on the Indivisibility of Canada* and during the campaign itself, Quebecers and other Canadians were made aware of the consequences of rejecting an indivisibility clause for Canada's constitution, they might all think twice. Quebecers like other Canadians are logical people. They know that if they are not in favour of an indivisible country, they must be in favour of a divisible one, and they will be prepared to examine, rationally, cooly, without resort to apocalyptic comparisons to Chechnya or Bosnia, the terms and conditions of that divisibility. Some of those basic terms, as we in the Equality Party see them, I've tried to outline for you tonight. There must be strict adherence to the rule of law in Canada, because the rule of law is the basis of democracy. There can be no tolerance of a UDI from any province in Canada, no repudiation of national debt or of Ottawa's fiduciary responsibilities to native peoples — in short, no independence without Canadian consent.

Finally and most importantly, there must no double standard on divisibility. If Canada is divisible, so is Quebec. If Quebec is indivisible, so is Canada. Ottawa must never veer from the fundamental democratic principle of 'consent to be governed' and so must reaffirm now the rights of loyal Canadians, already protected under the constitution, to remain Canadian — territorially part of Canada — in the areas where they form majorities come what may. Once these terms and conditions are laid down, I am confident Quebecers and their fellow citizens will see that the best Canada is one Canada, from sea to sea to sea, whole and indivisible. Securing that precious heritage should constitute our national New Year's resolution.

*T*he repercussions of the Moot Court Rally *were enormous. Partition, adopted by Equality as far back as 1991 as a poison pill policy in the event of a Quebec UDI, became stunningly and speedily popular. As early as February of 1996, polls suggested it was the preferred mainstream Canadian strategy against secession. Books appeared on the subject, vindicating EP members Bill Shaw and Lionel Albert's prescient* Partition: the Price of Quebec Independence, *universally panned by Quebec's 'right-thinking' set from its first publication in late 1979. With Equality and the* Special Committee's *help, Denzil Spence, Mayor of Allumette Island East in the Ottawa Valley Pontiac County, began the "Staying Canadian" municipalities movement, despite opposition from Quebec Liberal incumbents at all levels. Increasing pressure was placed on federal Liberals to defend the constitution of Canada, something it had been reluctant to do during the referendum. A week after the* Moot Court Rally *federal ministers were all talking about the divisibility of Quebec; Allan Rock, Justice Minister, had announced a new federal insistence on the 'rule of law;' Stéphane Dion was demanding clarifications from the PQ about whether it would try to use force to effect a UDI, and Lucien Bouchard had declared partition "illegal" and Quebec "indivisible," though, he added, Canada was divisible because it "was not a real country." The usual voices of appeasement and capitulation, however, greeted the* Moot Court Rally *with predictable disdain.*

Quick Spread of Partition Idea Should Worry All of Quebec

by Don Macpherson:
reprinted from the Gazette
January 23, 1996

I f only in terms of attendance, Sunday's meeting at the McGill law school of the burgeoning anglophone "partition" movement was a phenomenal success. A half-hour before the scheduled start, people were already being turned away at the entrance because there was no more space inside. The crowd spilled over from the 300-seat moot court, usually used for mock trials, into 3 classrooms. They crammed two lobbies, standing shoulder-to-shoulder for nearly three hours following the proceedings on television screens. The turnout showed how much of a sudden craze partition has become among English-speaking Quebecers in the less than three months since the referendum.

Like a drowning person grasping at flotsam, anglophones have latched onto the hope that Canada would only allow Quebec to secede if its federalist parts remained part of Canada. The crowd appeared to be almost exclusively English-speaking. The event was conducted mainly in English.

The meeting also succeeded in drawing francophone attention; it was carried live on RDI, Radio-Canada's all-news television channel. But the exposure probably killed whatever slim chance the idea of partition had of getting the support of francophones, especially the federalists who live in the very areas that would be broken off from the rest of Quebec. The list of speakers was dominated by anglophone personalities generally reputed in the francophone community to be hostile to French-speaking Quebec. They included *Gazette* columnist William Johnson, *Financial Post* editor Diane Francis and several prominent members and supporters of the English-rights Equality Party, including its leader, Keith Henderson. Equality members organized the meeting. And the party seems fully in control of the partition movement, which may at least temporarily restore the political relevance it had lost.

But Equality is not the only party whose interest in partition may be partly partisan. The organizers also invited a representative of the pro-partition federal Reform Party, which may be seeking a toehold in English Quebec as well as to exploit anti-Quebec sentiment in English-speaking Canada. Except for the large turnout, the meeting bore the characteristics of recent Equality meetings, especially the self-gratifying stridency.

Armchair patriot Francis called on Canada to resist separation to the last Quebec federalist in an escalating game of political chicken with the sovereignists, then scurried out of the meeting before it ended to catch the last flight back to the safety of Toronto. And if it comes down to a choice between living in a sovereign Quebec or in a loyalist enclave under the likes of McGill constitutional lawyer Stephen Scott, the anglo answer to Pierre Bourgault, taking one's chances with the sovereignists starts to look pretty good. The self-appointed Minister of Truth said opinion leaders, "including the media," must "speak firmly with one voice" and "work tirelessly with one mind" or be "discredited and driven from office as soon as possible." Yikes. And he unpleasantly fantasized about "chopping Quebec to bits" through partition with a combination of relish and near hostility.

Most of the speakers barely acknowledged the opinions, sensibilities, and very existence of francophones, including those who would be left clinging to Scott's hacked-off body parts, except to try to bludgeon them into loving Canada with threats to dismember Quebec. Still, whatever one may think of the would-be Ian Paisleys who would express their love of Canada by giving it a Northern Ireland of its own (as if it doesn't have enough problems already), it would be a mistake for francophones to dismiss them out of hand. For the spontaneous, wildfire-spread of the partition idea at the anglophone grassroots is a symptom of a malaise, the alienation and isolation of Quebec's English-speaking community, as well as its state of collective near-panic. It shows that the rosy assumptions of sovereignists, that those anglophones who haven't already joined the exodus out of Quebec have come to terms with sovereignty and would go along quietly with it, are wrong. And these are serious problems for Quebec as a whole.

*T*he most effective strategy against a separatist UDI was the municipalities initiative, Stephen Scott's brainchild, first successfully introduced by Pontiac county Mayor Denzil Spence. By dint of the superb grassroots efforts of the United Quebec Federalists, and despite the opposition of the region's péquiste and Quebec Liberal mayors alike, Mayor Spence managed to get the Municipal Regional Council of the Pontiac to agree to a declaration stating that, in the event of a UDI, the Pontiac would remain in Canada. With the help of Howard Galganov's Quebec Political Action Committee, 12,000 people gathered on the slopes of Parliament Hill in June '96 to celebrate the delivery of that declaration to the federal government, though no Liberal party officials were on hand to receive it. In August '96 Equality organized a meeting of all pro-Plan B groups, the first meeting of the Coalition for Canadian Unity, which adopted the municipalities initiative as its top priority. The movement spread to central and western Montreal, where it encountered the same initial hostility from elected officials that Denzil Spence had contended with in the Pontiac. Chief among these opponents of the 'Staying Canadian' resolutions was the mayor of Westmount and member of the Quebec Liberal party, Peter Trent.

Nervous-Nellies Dismiss Municipal Referendum Idea

by Keith Henderson:
reprinted from The Financial Post
November, 1996

Two votes are in — two thumping majorities for pro-Canada cities giving citizens a right to state whether or not they'd prefer to stay in Canada before a PQ inspired referendum is held and regardless of the results. Last week it was Montreal suburb Côte St.-Luc. This week Hampstead. Add these declarations to the one the mayors of the entire municipal region of Pontiac made last spring and Quebec separatists can be counted on tearing their hair out. After all, the resolutions just turn the tables on what the PQ (and the me-too Quebec Liberals) have been arguing for years. "Quebecers have the right to self-determination," they've said. By that token so do Canadians, and if the federal government abdicates its responsibilities by not giving all of us a say in the future of our country, some of us will get one through our municipal councils. Rupture abhors a vacuum.

We can thank a coalition of 18 Quebec unity groups for this initiative, led by two people who want to keep a place for young Canadians in Quebec, Hampstead city councillor, Anthony Housefather, 26, and 25 year-old mother of two, Miriam McCormick, a doctoral philosophy student at McGill. "We can accept what has happened and silently watch this city diminish, or we can persuade people to reverse the decline — to make it a place people come to rather than leave," she said. McCormick believes the best way to reverse things, apart from recovering Canadians' civil rights in Quebec, is to get secession off the provincial agenda, by letting separatists know the true consequences of their dream. Partitioning Canada will lead to a partitioned Quebec.

For Housefather, the best Quebec referendum is no referendum, most probably assured by telling the PQ there won't be only one. To the nervous-nellies wringing their hands about whether the kind of resolution he proposed was legal, Housefather got off the rejoinder of the week: "Why is it legal to have as Canada's official opposition the *Bloc Québécois,* dedicated to the destruction of our country, but it's not legal for Quebec municipalities to state they want to stay Canadian?" That earned him a standing ovation in Hampstead.

Housefather and McCormick aren't without some high-powered friends. Back in the days when he wasn't singing the praises of the distinct society and Bill 101, Stéphane Dion remarked that municipalities may be the best jurisdiction to use to gauge the public's 'Staying Canadian' sentiment, a view echoed in Patrick Monahan's C.D. Howe Institute study, *Coming to Terms with Plan B.*

But high-powered adversaries abound, centred around what one editorialist called Westmount's Quebec "Liberal Party/cocktail party circuit." Mayor Peter F. Trent, head of the Council of Suburban mayors, is one. He thinks municipal referenda are defeatist and a waste of time. "Non-francophones need to get out and go after the soft-federalist underbelly of the francophone population." Of course, Trent fails to explain what happens if they won't listen. It's only a 'freckle theory' anyway, he argues. Little pro-Canada dots on the map won't produce territory continguous to Canada. Here Trent ignores the fact that Daniel Johnson's own riding voted NO and attaches most of the other NO ridings, including 80% of the island of Montreal, to Ontario. (Besides, municipal referenda are indicators, not boundary setting mechanisms.) Finally Trent says it's "up to the feds to have predetermined the map of post-referendum Quebec." But he won't tell us what happens if they don't. For Peter Trent municipal referenda are just cathartic exercises, uselessly preaching to the converted. For Housefather and McCormick, if someone's setting fires in the neighbourhood, the order of the day's an insurance policy.

*B*y the fall of '97, 43 Quebec municipalities had adopted unity resolutions. Denzil Spence had crossed the Ottawa River and secured the endorsement of virtually all of eastern Ontario for a strong 'Staying Canadian' position. Mayors and reeves representing nearly 1.5 million Ontario residents had lined up behind their fellow Canadians in Quebec. One of the high-water marks of the movement was a May 21st rally in Ville St. Laurent, the largest federalist rally of the on-going '97 federal election campaign, during which Guy Bertrand announced he would be taking the resolutions to the Supreme Court as part of his intervention in the UDI reference case. Only a few weeks before, bowing to grassroots pressure, Westmount's Peter Trent had introduced his own unity resolution, though true to form, it was among the weakest of the 40 adopted.

Westmount Municipal Rally Speech

by Keith Henderson:
May 7, 1997

L adies and gentlemen, why are we having an election now, only three and a half years into the government's mandate? We know the usual answers. Because Liberals want approval for the course they've set. Because they're high in the polls, and the opposition is divided. But I'm going to suggest another answer to you tonight, one I think is the real answer. We are having an election now because the Liberals are far enough away from the Supreme Court decision on Separation that's coming in 9 months — an historic decision, perhaps one of the most important in modern Canadian history, a decision that may precipitate a provincial election here in Quebec, and conceivably Referendum III. The governing Liberal party does not want that issue on the table during a federal election campaign. They prefer to avoid it, to skate around it, to get a mandate from you without talking about it, so they can be free to act however they choose when the time comes.

Nor are they alone in that desire. No party wants to talk about Unity issue. To be fair Conservative Leader Jean Charest did mention the possibility that parts of Quebec may stay in Canada while the rest secedes is "on the table" after a YES vote. But be careful. Here's how he put it: "As much as separatists would like to walk away from it, as much as others would like ironclad guarantees of a right to remain in Canada, not one group or the other will get the answer they're looking for."

Not one group or the other will get the answer they're looking for. I'm sorry, Mr. Charest, but I'm very troubled by that way of putting things. Does that mean loyal Canadians deserve no more than separatists? That the one group is equivalent to the other? No. This cannot be. That is not acceptable. Canadians in Quebec want guarantees. Canadians expect guarantees, and as citizens we have the right to guarantees. Those who've been most loyal to Canadian ideals, who've twice voted NO to break up the country, we who've been at the cutting edge of a debate that has gone on too long, who've lived its traumas and costs in moved children and lost values, we the people to whom all Canadians should be grateful for our fight and our votes, we citizens, hundreds of whom are gathered here tonight, deserve better than to be told we might not have the protection of our Canadian government against the depredations of separatists. We have been loyal to our country, Mr. Charest. Let our country be loyal to us.

But has Mr. Chrétien done any better? I believe Mr. Chrétien and the Liberal party of Canada have been ducking this issue for too long. Why do I think that? They had the Lesage judgment before the '95 referendum stating the PQ project was illegal and unconstitutional. Mr. Chrétien never used the judgement in his referendum campaign, never talked about it, never raised it, and Liberals voted against letting Guy Bertrand and myself raise it in the campaign too.

In December '96 fully one year after the referendum, Mr. Chrétien was asked by a concerned Gaspé resident in a CBC Townhall meeting if he could expect the help of his federal government in the event of a YES vote. Do you know what Mr. Chrétien answered? First he answered: "That's a hypothetical question." To his credit the Gaspé man persisted. "How can it be hypothetical," he asked, "when there was only 1% difference between YES and NO in '95 and Referendum III promised?" The moderator Peter Mansbridge intervened. "Just a Yes or a No answer, Mr. Prime Minister," said Mansbridge.

Now do you know what Mr. Chrétien said? "Well, you can always move," he said. Imagine. "You can always move!" I would have expected such a comment from separatists, not from my Prime Minister. Mr. Chrétien, I have news for you. We're not moving. *Nous y sommes. Nous y restons. C'est le Canada ici.* And there's the beauty of those pro-Canada resolutions adopted by all sorts of municipalities in Quebec — those resolutions that demand that the federal government do the *minimum* that a national government must do for its citizens, to do moreover what the French version of our national anthem promises Canada *will* do, that is to say to protect our homes and our rights, to assure us that we will continue to form part of this splendid country, come what may.

So Mr. Chrétien, Mr. Manning, Mr. Charest, Ms. McDonough — I will not pose the question to Mr. Duceppe who has already abandoned Canada — what will you do if there is a YES the next time round? What will you do? You have asked us to have confidence in you. What will you do for us, the good, loyal Canadians of Quebec? Tell us. Tell us straight, and tell us before June 2nd, not after.

Ladies and gentlemen, I believe what Quebec's Canadians want is an end to evasions, to indirection, to confusion and refusal to answer questions. We want an end to ostrich politics that have characterized this country for the past 20 years. Can there be a greater question posed in the history of a nation than whether that nation will continue to exist? Imagine a federal campaign over the next month during which this question is never addressed. That is inconceivable. That cannot be allowed to happen. We, the people in this room, and outside in our towns and cities, through our representatives closest to us — here at the municipal level, where our property values are determined and the safety of our streets is kept, we must raise this debate and demand answers to our questions. This is not radicalism. This is not divisiveness. This is not to set English against French or to threaten anyone. This is simple prudence. It is simple common sense. Mr. Prime Minister, whoever you may be on June 2nd, what will you do in two years' time if there's a YES? Tell us. Tell us now, and then we'll see, based on your answers, whether we'll trust you with our votes.

I think we can be forgiven for being confused. Mr. Prime Minister you have said on occasions that you would respect a YES vote. What did that mean? Did that mean that any province can secede? That if Albertans suddenly got tired of sharing their wealth with other Canadians they could vote to leave, break Canada in two and the federal government would simply acquiesce? If that is not the case and Alberta could not do that, why can Quebec? And if Quebec cannot do that, why have you not said so more clearly and more often?

Mr. Prime Minister, you have said that a YES represented an irrevocable choice of a country — an *irrevocable* choice. If the choice was irrevocable and Quebecers chose twice to remain Canadian, why would you participate in a third referendum on the same subject?

Mr. Prime Minister you have said the question had to be clear and won by a sufficient majority. Why then is Canada the only place in the world that allows separatist forces to determine the question, count the ballots, set the threshold for victory, the schedule of negotiations, and threaten a possible Unilateral Declaration of Independence? Why did you participate so passively in such referendums, not once but twice? Why would you participate in a third on the same conditions?

Mr. Prime Minister, you have stated that all Canadians would have their word to say on the future of their country, should ever there be a YES. Why have you not said how? Would it be through the auspices of a pan-Canadian referendum? An election? Tell us please.

Mr. Prime Minister you have implied that "if Canada is divisible, so is Quebec," but you have never stated whether in fact Canada *is divisible,* and if it is, under what terms and conditions. Would you not think it better to have an indivisible Canada? If you do not, could you tell us why? Would you be prepared to let Canadians themselves decide that question? And if on the other hand Canada is divisible, do you think loyal areas of a seceding province should have the right to stay Canadian? 59% of Canadians think so. Do you? If you do, would you make that pledge to us now, before the June 2nd election?

These are the sorts of questions our municipalities resolutions will force upon the table. This is the debate Canadians must have. Now is the time to ask these questions, when our federal politicians seek our mandate. Here is the place, in Montreal, in pro-Canada Quebec, where 2 referendums have been won, for this debate to begin. There is no better. Municipal leaders in 26 towns and cities in Quebec have already taken the lead, in Hampstead, Cote St. Luc, Dollard, Dorval, Pointe-Claire, Beaconsfield, Mount Royal and in the Pontiac. More are on the way. I am proud of them. Are Westmounters any less Canadian? I want to be proud of my Westmount City Council too.

Ladies and gentlemen, I will conclude on this note. One day before the election, on June 1st of this year, Canada will open the Confederation Bridge, a 13 kilometre span across the Northumberland Strait linking the provinces of New Brunswick and P.E.I for the first time in history. Some may dispute it, but I think that is a major achievement. Now I ask you.

What good will that bridge be if in two years the land bridge between the Maritimes and Ontario which is Quebec is broken? What good will that Confederation Bridge be if our federal government allows the Canada we know from sea to sea to be divided in three? Would the government of Canada ever allow such a thing, what André Laurendeau forty years ago described as "a geographical absurdity which Canadians would never permit?"

I do believe, whatever the results of future referendums, dividing Canada in 3 must never happen. Our Prime Minister-to-be must promise that it will never happen, that whatever the future brings, east and west will remain territorially linked. Canada must never be the Pakistan of North America. Never. And so our Prime Minister-to-be must recognize that these municipal resolutions we are asking our City Councillors to adopt are the first span in that land link. We will build it, span by span, until it includes, with certainty, the whole of Quebec. Already in the midst of our efforts, support for separation is dropping. We will enlist more municipalities, more territories, more NO areas, French and English together, in the strong conviction that our 'Staying Canadian' fight is the Maritimes' 'Staying Canadian' fight. It is all of Canada's 'Staying Canadian' fight. Ladies and gentlemen, we must tell our Prime Minister-to-be that we Canadians in Quebec — for 30 years too long on the cutting edge of this debate, here on this territory — *we* are Canada's Confederation Bridge. You cannot abandon us.

❖

*A*s they had often done in the past, opponents of the 'Staying Canadian' movement tried to tar its proponents as fomenters of violence and civil war. Calls came for the 'partitionist' movement to run candidates in the '97 federal election, taunting sorts of suggestions which Equality determined to ignore.

It's Time for Partitionists To Put Up or Shut Up

by Don MacPherson:
reprinted from the Gazette
April 19, 1997

Where are the partitionists? Since the last referendum, there's been a lot of talk in the English-speaking community about partitioning Quebec so that its federalist parts remain in Canada, regardless of the outcome of another sovereignty referendum. Polls indicate a majority of anglophones favour partition. Well, now it's time to turn the talk into votes and, if possible, elected representatives. A federal election is expected to be called in a little over a week. It will be the first province-wide vote since the referendum, and the first opportunity since then for the whole English-speaking community to make its voice heard where it counts — in the polling booths. The campaigning is already under way.

So, where are the partitionist candidates? English-rights crusader Howard Galganov has announced he's running as an independent candidate in Mount Royal riding against Liberal Sheila Finestone. But, while he frequently allies himself with the partitionists, he's not a partitionist himself. Are the partitionists even going to run candidates?

The partitionists have certainly been active recently — at the municipal level, where they've succeeded in getting the city councils of several predominantly non-francophone Montreal suburbs to adopt "unity" resolutions. It has been an effective strategy, because it has allowed the partitionists to concentrate their efforts and resources on one municipality at a time and to create an impression of gathering momentum and growing support. But while the municipal resolutions might reassure some residents, it's a false sense of security. What the partitionists need, and what they lack right now, is a firm commitment from Ottawa and the other provinces that they would insist on partition as a condition of consenting to Quebec's secession. What will be the position of the next federal government? Will it be committed to insisting on partition? Will Quebec partitionists at least be represented in the next Parliament?

The incumbent Liberals, notably Prime Minister Chrétien and his minister of intergovernmental affairs, Stéphane Dion, have toyed publicly with partition on occasion. But they've stopped short of committing a Liberal government to insisting on partition as part of its "Plan B" for dealing with a pro-sovereignty vote in Quebec. Only one of the parties now represented in Parliament is in favour of partition: the Reform Party. But its chances of forming the next government appear slim. And its chances of electing candidates in Quebec, even in predominantly anglophone ridings, appear just as slim. The pro-partition plank in Reform's platform would come with a lot of other planks on language and social issues that would be a tough sell to English-speaking Quebecers, who tend to be small-l liberals. A 'home-grown' Quebec party such as a federal Equality Party might stand a better chance.

In some ways, this election is shaping up like the 1989 provincial vote in which Equality elected four members even though it had no money or organization. In that election, many English-speaking voters were alienated from the Quebec Liberal Party, which they had traditionally supported. And the polls assured them that even if they split their votes, there was no risk of a separatist government being elected. Similarly, going into the federal campaign, there's no chance of Quebec separatists forming the next federal government (even in Canada, some political absurdities are impossible.) And anglophone support for the federal Liberals could be soft because of their performance in the referendum.

Right now, this federal election looks to be the last one before another Quebec sovereignty referendum, and also the last chance for Quebec partitionists to ensure that they have a voice in the Parliament that might be called upon to negotiate the terms of separation. In the *Gazette* last Monday, partitionist spokesman Brent Tyler argued in favour of putting pressure on Liberal candidates, in particular, to endorse partition. But the most effective form of pressure on any candidate is the danger of losing votes. For the sake of their own credibility, it's time for the partitionists to show how much political muscle there is behind all their talk.

Equality Won't Run in Federal Election

by Keith Henderson:
reprinted from the Gazette
April 23, 1997

The Unity Coalition has had considerable success with its municipal 'Staying Canadian' resolutions lately, resolutions intended to assert Canadians' constitutional right to the protection of their national government against secessionist threats, but which separatist sympathizers have dubbed "partitionist." They're not, of course. Separatists are the true partitionists, in the sense that separatists actually *want* secession and territorial division. Loyal Canadians don't. A further measure of the difference is that the whole question of partition would disappear tomorrow if separatists stopped threatening Canada's very existence, advice Bouchard and Duceppe are obviously in no hurry to accept.

Faced with PQ-BQ obduracy, their refusal to accept the results of two referendums, and their persistent threat of a third, Canadians in Quebec have had no choice but to organize to defend their interests. Hence the first Unity Coalition meeting in July 1996 held at the request of the Equality Party, its founding members consisting of Equality, *The Quebec Committee for Canada, The Special Committee for Canadian Unity, the Quebec Political Action Committee,* and the Pontiac region's *United Quebec Federalists.*

Despite Equality's presence, the Unity Coalition is wholly non-partisan. Any group, political or otherwise, that shares Coalition aims can join, and presence in the Unity Coalition in no way implies endorsement of the Equality Party. At that July '96 meeting the Coalition set two key targets for subsequent action — the defence of Canadian minority language rights and the 'Staying Canadian' municipalities resolutions. Efforts on the latter front have been so effective, they've provoked reactions from both separatists and soft federalists alike.

PQ Municipal Affairs Minister Rémy Trudel lead the separatist charge last January when he declared municipalities had no legal competence to conduct referendums on whether their citizens would like to stay in Canada, an absurdly hypocritical position given the PQ's penchant for asking Quebecers unconstitutional questions. Throughout, various separatists have raised the issue of force, continually arguing that should the territorial integrity of Quebec ever be threatened, violence would erupt. Ed Bantey is only the latest to join the parade. "...Given Quebec's timid 'no way' to partition, force is the only means Ottawa would have to implement the partitionist dream," he wrote.

Say again? Which 'timid' type would fire the first shot? Lucien Bouchard? The *Sureté du Québec?* Some nut case? We've had 30 years of partitionist talk from separatists like Bantey, whose dream is to go beyond the rule of law and cut Canada in two, something André Laurendeau called "an absurdity" which Canadians would never accept. Yet heaven help us if a serious federalist commentator were ever to write the reverse: "Given Ottawa's timid 'no way' to separation, force is the only means Quebec would have to implement the secessionist dream." Would Ed Bantey take these words as a cool statement of fact? Or would he be howling outrage about federalists imputing nasty motives to separatists?

Don Macpherson's "It's time for partitionists to put up or shut up" is at once more serious and more worrisome. MacPherson is only partly right in saying what the 'Staying Canadian' team needs and what it lacks right now "is a firm commitment from Ottawa and the other provinces that they would insist on partition as a condition of consenting to Quebec's secession." What the 'Staying Canadian' team really needs is a commitment to the indivisibility of Canada, the touchstone of all mature democracies. Only if Canadians agree that the country they fought to build and maintain is indeed divisible should there be the kind of commitment Macpherson talks about, not just to reassure loyalists, but to place the terms and conditions of divisibility clearly on the map so all Canadians, including separatists, know what they're facing should we continue down the partitionist road that secessionists themselves have paved.

Where Macpherson goes wrong is when he appears to counsel the Equality Party to run candidates in the federal campaign to secure that position. 'Come on out and fight,' he seems to be saying, 'and if you lose, shut up and go away,' a strategy that seems calculated to have those who believe in 'Staying Canadian' throw away their hard won credibility rather than build on it. Most people haven't entirely given up on their federal representatives on this issue, the way they're rapidly giving up on their provincial ones. Having fought for its principles before (to much sneering and derision), the worst thing Equality could do at this point is squander its hard earned resources on a fight it's not positioned to win.

Macpherson also goes wrong when he says: "This federal election looks to be the last ... chance for Quebec partitionists to ensure that they have a voice in the Parliament that might be called upon to negotiate the terms of separation." 'Staying Canadian' types have to keep their eye on the ball. Using the bulwark of the municipalities resolutions, they must pressure the federal government to do its duty to them — to defend their citizenship against the depredations of separatists. But the true prize is Referendum III. It is imperative that unconditional Canadians run the next NO campaign. Daniel Johnson, who made such a mess of things the last time, is poised to suffer one of the worst electoral defeats the Quebec Liberal Party has faced, given his own shortcomings and the outrageous skewing of Quebec's electoral map in favour of rural, separatist ridings. The prospect of strong Canadians in and around Equality forming the next official opposition in Quebec is not impossible. Fifteen seats may do it.

That is the fight Equality must position itself to win, for it will change the complexion of the softball, zip-your-mouth NO campaign Johnson ran last time into the articulate, passionate, daring campaign Canadians expected. With territory and the rule of law on the table, YES support will drop. Those who want to stay Canadian must see to it. That way the next federal parliament won't be negotiating the terms of separation. It won't have to.

The Price of Partition

by Don Macpherson:
reprinted from the Gazette
May 27, 1997

I f Canada is divisible, so is Quebec. That's the partitionist mantra, to be repeated over and over again until all fears of Quebec's separation from Canada vanish from the mind. It sounds so simple. Quebec's present territory would be divided after a YES vote in another sovereignty referendum and federalist areas would remain part of Canada. Federalist Quebecers could 'Stay Canadian,' another partitionist slogan, without having to move. Life in, say, the West Island suburbs would stay the same, except that separatism and the separatists would simply go away, as if at a wave of the federalist version of Lucien Bouchard's magic wand. No need to move, to sell the house, find a new job.

If Canada is divisible, so is Quebec. As a principle and a tit-for-tat debating point, it's unassailable, bulletproof. But it does not begin to answer questions about exactly how Quebec's present territory would be divided after a YES vote in another referendum on sovereignty, so that federalist areas of its present territory would remain part of Canada. And the answers to some of those questions make partition appear so impractical and costly that it is not likely to happen.

Let's start with the question of whether partition would lead to violence. A touchy question, to be sure, but one that partitionists themselves have brought up. The Equality Party, which is prominent in the partitionist movement, certainly seems to think that violence is a possibility. Equality's official policy on partition "requests and requires the government of Canada to provide the support, economically, materially, and if necessary *militarily* (my italics), to protect 'Canadian Federalist Quebec' against any attempted interdictions by the new separatist state to suborn 'Canadian Federalist Quebec' into its domain."

This makes Equality, to my knowledge, the only political party in Canada, federalist or separatist, that, as a matter of official policy, advocates or even contemplates the use of force in connection with an attempted secession by Quebec. (And, yes, that includes the *Parti Québécois,* though there has been some sabre-rattling by such individual *Péquistes* as Quebec's Louis Napoléon, Jacques Brassard.) But for a partitionist party, perhaps it's only prudent to provide for the possible use of force. After all, two examples of partition that leap immediately to mind are those of West Virginia and Northern Ireland, both of which took civil wars to create.

This raises two questions for the partitionists: how many examples are there in history of territories that have been partitioned between two countries without involving violence? And is the use of force justified to achieve partition? (Yes, yes, I know:

the separatists started all this by proposing a unilateral declaration of independence. But the question of who started what might not matter a great deal to those who found themselves in the midst of violence associated with either a UDI or partition.)

While we wait for the partitionists' answers to those questions, it's worth noting that the prospective future citizens of 'Canadian Federalist Quebec' seem reluctant to see their neighbourhoods turned into new Belfasts, with their children and grandchildren playing around armoured vehicles and going to school under the protection of armed soldiers. In the recent COMPAS INC. survey for Southam News, even in the staunchly federalist regions of Montreal's West Island, the Outaouais and the Eastern Townships, majorities of respondents said the use of Canada's armed forces to divide Quebec would not be justified. Perhaps, in a future poll, respondents might also be asked whether they would be less likely to support partition if they thought it might involve violence.

But enough talk of violence for now. Indeed, the partitionists themselves can put an end to that talk once and for all, simply by declaring that the use of force to achieve partition would not be justified (and while we're on the subject, the sovereignists might similarly clarify their own position.) It's always possible, at least theoretically, that partition could be negotiated peacefully between Quebec and Canada. That, however, still leaves other questions about partition unanswered — questions about whether it would be in Canada's interests to seek partition.

The Spectre of Armed Conflict

by Keith Henderson:
reprinted from the Gazette
May 1997

When Equality first raised the question of a separatist UDI in a Toronto press conference as early as the spring of '94, the *Gazette's* Don Macpherson reported that we'd gone to Toronto and enlisted the support of influential and worried Canadians like Michael Bliss, Jack Granatstein, and Kenneth McNaught "to raise the spectre of armed conflict" and advocate the "permanent military occupation of Quebec to keep Quebec in Canada." Macpherson was wrong. What we really said in Toronto was this: "Would Jacques Parizeau and Lucien Bouchard use the police to enforce the (essentially illegal and unconstitutional) decrees of a newly 'sovereign' provincial government? That is the *prior* question to which none of us has had an answer," we said. "Until we get one, we cannot reasonably enter into the subject of force or coercion. If Parizeau and Bouchard *do* use force, i.e. the police — and let them say so if this is their intent — then we would expect the federal government to use whatever means are necessary to protect the rights and safety of law-abiding Canadian citizens."

Macpherson was wrong about Equality in 1994, and he continues to be wrong now. What he can't seem to get it into his head is that separatists are instigating the fight and threatening to break the law, not the Equality Party. It is Lucien Bouchard and Jacques Parizeau who are calling for the partitioning of Canada as a good in itself, when Equality simply prefers an indivisible Canada and seeks protection of our citizens' rights to remain part of our own country. It is *Péquistes* like Bernard Landry who actively investigate the possibilities of the formation of a Quebec army and leaders like Bouchard who help send seditious faxes to Canadian army units in Quebec inviting them to transfer their loyalties to the post-UDI new state of Quebec — "treason" in most other countries, as former general Lewis MacKenzie himself stated. And who does Don Macpherson continue to blame for "raising the spectre of armed conflict?" His tiny and beloved Eeks.

True, Macpherson quoted Equality policy accurately. We do "request and require the government of Canada to provide the support, economically and materially, and if necessary militarily, to protect 'Canadian Federalist Quebec' against any attempted interdictions by the new separatist state to suborn 'Canadian Federalist Quebec' into its domain." But what does that mean? Simply that in the event of a UDI, Canadians in Quebec will not be kidnapped into a new rogue state. We expect the protection of our federal government against treasonous, seditious, and unlawful behaviour on the part of our provincial government. If Bouchard sends a post-

UDI directive to Westmount's mayor Peter Trent ordering him to remit all deductions at source to Quebec and not to Ottawa, Trent is on record stating that he would continue to abide by the constitution of Canada and remit them to Ottawa. If Bouchard uses the police to give force and effect to his illegal directives, as Jacques Brassard has threatened to do, Mayor Trent would be entitled to the protection of his federal government in the exercise of his duties. So would we all. This is not a radical concept. It is called upholding the rule of law, the first obligation of a democracy. Not to do so, the course Macpherson advocates, is to submit to anarchy and blackmail, the cowardly course, which history has taught the clearer-minded among us always leads to more disorder and pain in the long run.

Macpherson implies that Equality has never answered the question of "exactly how Quebec's present territory would be divided after a YES vote." That too, of course, is false. Driven by secessionists and a craven federal government to choose the lesser of two evils, swallowing a UDI whole or partitioning Quebec, most Canadians would opt for the latter. The easiest way would be for Canada simply to retain all those provincial ridings that voted NO, though poll by poll examination in some areas might reflect people's choice of country more accurately. Canada's maritime interests cannot be ignored, and the territorial link to the Atlantic provinces would have to be secured. The express desires of the aboriginal people to stay in Canada would also have to respected.

Macpherson pretends such arrangements can never be arrived at through negotiation, but history is replete with examples to the contrary, the Saar, Alsace-Lorraine, the Swiss canton of Jura being but a few. If this were not the case, how could Macpherson have witnessed 30 years of separatist threats to the territorial integrity of Canada and never once have raised the possibility of Quebec secession turning Canada into North America's Ireland? The best news, however, is that politics is now the insurance business. No insurance salesmen will tell you that his policy will actually prevent a fire. But polls suggest the 'be prepared' policies of the 'Staying Canadian' movement and the Equality Party can and will prevent secession. The very *talk* of dividing Quebec, as secessionists wish to divide Canada, loses the separatists votes and consigns Macpherson's "spectre of armed conflict" to the closet, where it belongs.

In his Centaur speech last March premier Bouchard announced that he was "deeply troubled when I hear neighbours on the street next to mine" talking about partitioning Quebec. He later added that he was "heartened" to hear some federalists in Montreal raising arguments against partition. The conclusion is inescapable and should be conveyed to Don Macpherson and the *Gazette* with ribbons and maple leaves all over it. If you want to hearten separatists, criticize those who argue that Quebec is divisible. If you want to worry separatists, even "deeply trouble" them, join the 75% of Canadians who think separatists have no right to take loyal Canadians with them on their suicidal adventure.

*N*eedless to say, few if any of the clear questions Equality posed to the federal Liberals during the May '97 campaign were answered. Still, in some respects Ottawa has begun taking a firmer line against secession than ever before. Certainly poll results suggest a substantial majority of Canadians now favour partition, if necessary, and a strong anti-UDI position. Such results have heartened their fellow citizens in Quebec, who now see the separatists on the defensive for the first time in a decade or more. Dangers still abound, not the least of which surround the issue of the conduct of Referendum III, another of those key subjects upon which the federal Liberals remained exquisitely silent throughout the '97 election campaign.

UDI may not Need YES Vote

by Keith Henderson:
reprinted from The Financial Post
June 2, 1997

C ynical Canadian election strategists must be congratulating themselves. They've just led four federalist parties through a national campaign 6 months before the most momentous court decision in our history and succeeded in never once talking about what they would do afterwards. Ever fear. As vampires resurrect, so will the prospects of UDI over the months to come, and in ways few of us might predict.

Ex-premier Jacques Parizeau gave some hint of this two weeks back when he revealed that at the promptings of former French president Valérie Giscard d'Estaing he would have declared independence "within days" of a YES vote. Bouchard's subsequent loud disclaimers we can entirely discount, Bouchard himself having threatened much the same thing in Paris in '94. To forestall this disaster (which Chrétien should have foreseen long ago), the feds have belatedly gone to court, let it be known 50% +

1 doesn't cut it, and stated that they want a hand in the formulation of the future question. Here the problems only begin.

Take it as a given the courts will vindicate Ottawa. What then? A 'hate-that-foreign-court' Quebec election which Bouchard can win, preparations for Referendum III, and a Bouchard announcement that the feds will never co-write the question. True to form, the federaloid Quebec Liberals will side with the PQ. Should the complexion of the legislature not by then have changed (perish the thought), there will emerge another of those Stalinesque 'unanimous votes of the National Assembly' in this, the most divided of Canada's provinces. What does Ottawa do? Participate in Referendum III and confirm its own impotence? Boycott and encourage as much as half the potential NO votes to stay home, with results predictable at the polls and imponderable everywhere else? There would be chaos in Quebec. The Brinks trucks episode of the '70s would be a Santa Claus parade compared to what would occur. People would be calling for a halt to the entire gruesome spectacle. UDI awaits.

As Carl Friederich once put it, "The dictators of this century, following the example of Napoleon, have ... relied upon ... referendums or plebiscites for legitimizing their unconstitutional and anticonstitutional regimes." That's why the federal government owes us a *National Referendum Act* in which the terms and conditions of all referendums in Canada are spelled out. No provincial law that lets a referendum trigger its own coming into effect should be allowed. No referendum question a YES to which would affect the Constitution of Canada or federal prerogatives should be permitted without prior federal approval. The 'peace, order, and good government' of the country requires it — a federal constitutional responsibility thoroughly justified by what we may be about to live through. "Plainly," said Abraham Lincoln in his inaugural address of 1861, "the central idea of secession is the essence of anarchy... I trust this will not be regarded as a menace, but only as the declared purpose of the Union that it *will* constitutionally defend and maintain itself."

Don't for a moment think the possibility of a federal Referendum Act hasn't occurred to the heavy-hitters of the PQ. While purring over Slovakia's velvet divorce from the Czech Republic in his recent book, Jacques Parizeau let slip that he'd always been in favour of UDI based on the PQ's legislative majority in Quebec. "Voluntarily to renounce our commitment not to separate from Canada until we'd won a referendum would be to betray the mandate the people of Quebec had bestowed on its leaders. Unless, of course, we're forced. If Ottawa tries to make a Quebec referendum illegal... 'Those whom the gods would destroy, they first make mad.'"

The clear implication is that if Ottawa passed a 'National Referendum Act,' the PQ might return to the preferred Parizeau strategy of trying to destroy Canada with the hammer of a Quebec legislative majority. All things considered, however, that is a far better tool to force Bouchard to use than to submit to the indecencies of Referendum III based on the same rules as Referendum II. And should Bouchard wield the weapon and try an illegal and unconstitutional parliamentary UDI? The first thing the feds should do is tell him the legislative assembly of Quebec is a creature of the BNA Act and that if he should feel compelled to make seditious pronouncements, he will not make them in a Canadian legislature with the royal mace before him. Let him go to a local hotel. Better still, a tennis court. The mace belongs to Canada.

*T*he second major repercussion from the Moot Court meeting was the new emphasis, long overdue, on the processes of recognition surrounding a UDI and the rules governing it. Separatists, forced to abandon the theory of 'self-determination' of nations, once they were told it did not apply to Quebec, moved on to the doctrine of 'effective control,' the international equivalent of 'possession is nine-tenths of the law.' Here lay the real politik of UDI at its stark worst, even though secessionists only emphasize the diplomatic niceties of international recognition, the brass bands and red carpet receptions, never the painful process of securing that recognition in the first place. That process involves force, Stephen Scott's "original sin of states," something separatists rarely mention but were well aware of in the lead-up to the '95 referendum. How else to explain Lucien Bouchard's faxes to Quebec army units inviting them to "transfer their loyalty to new Quebec state" the day after a YES vote? How else to explain the separatists' obsession with France and the possibilities of instant French recognition for their UDI?

Claude Charron's: *The Partition of Quebec*

by Keith Henderson:
reprinted from The Financial Post
July 24, 1996

G ive CBC separatist Claude G. Charron credit. The cover of his book, *La Partition du Québec: de Lord Durham à Stéphane Dion* features Canada's carrion crows stealing little bits of the map of Quebec. The culprits? Constitutional expert Stephen Scott, author William Johnson, editor Diane Francis, Quebec City lawyer Guy Bertrand — the same flock that landed at McGill University's moot court last January 21 and with the help of the *Special Committee for Canadian Unity* exploded the whole partition question onto the national agenda. At least the separatists know who their enemies are.

Give Charron credit too for some fascinating historical research. Few of us 'staying Canadian' types knew back in 1830s that Lord Durham contemplated not what eventually came to pass, a union of Upper and Lower Canada, but a three part division — Upper Canada for anglos, bilingual middle Canada for mongrels, and *pure laine* Lower

Canada for the *Québécois*. More fascinating still, the frontiers of Durham's mongrel middle Canada correspond 150 years later almost exactly to the portions of Quebec that voted NO in the last referendum, west Quebec along the Ottawa, the region around the Island of Montreal, and the eastern townships. *Plus ça change....*

There the praises for *La Partition* end. This is, after all, a separatist diatribe, complete with all the woolly-minded *Québécois* double-talk Canadians have come to know and love over the past 30 years. Take, for example, the definition of terms. Those who want to stay Canadian on the territory of Quebec, come what may, Charron labels 'partitionists,' proponents of an idea pioneered, he tells us, by the British, who supervised three 20th century partitions in Ireland, Palestine, and India, all associated to some degree with violence and ethnic cleansing. These whom others might simply call loyal Canadians, Charron at first calls Rhodesians. Then he asks: "How could we not see in partitionist discourse the stench of such ideas as *lebensraum* and talk of the superiority of one people and culture over other peoples, the discourse of the thirties?" Loyal Canadians as Nazis, anyone?

Separatists, of course, are not partitionists. That would be confusing. They are simply erstwhile hewers of wood and drawers of water, put upon by Canada, prisoners of a constitution not of their choosing, not recognized alas as a colonized people (because too rich, too autonomous, and too developed) and so without the right to declare their independence unilaterally, a 'wanna-be' colony at best, but then as such, perhaps still able to claim the true perks of colonial status — a home grown revolution and a seat at the UN. Incredibly, Charron writes: "Perhaps it's time to ask if the good old theories of Memmi on colonialism wouldn't be the best remedy for the current impasse. After all, if we could recognize that Quebec hadn't escaped being a colony...."

Were it so recognized, of course, in the world according to Charron, Quebec City would have the right to impose its will on all those who lived on the territory. Basing himself on the 5 experts in international law who testified before the Bélanger-Campeau Commission, Charron declares in the event of secession: "Canada would be divisible and Quebec not. This stems from the principle that the country consists of two nations and that the smaller of the two, Quebec, has the right to secede without its minorities, whether aboriginal, anglophone, or allophone, having the same right in return."

Ignore for a moment the fact that the experts said no such thing. Quebec has no right to secede. Neither does anybody else. Consider instead how Charron sees secession taking place. Quebec, he says, after a YES vote will simply declare itself independent and count on international recognition to secure its status. Everyone, including France and the Americans, of course, would race to recognize the new nation. Then, if anyone else tried to secede, Quebec would invoke international law to prevent them. The moral? Separatists can flout the law and confront the international community with a *fait accompli.* Federalists have to play by the rules.

In a classic case of pot calling kettle black, Charron spends much of his book accusing Canadians living in Quebec of an addiction to armies and force — crypto-Serbs all. What he fails to mention in his rogue-state analysis of accession to independence is the criteria Americans (among others) use to determine which breakaway states to recognize. The breakaway state must demonstrate effective control over its territory and expel all competing law. That means pulling loyal Canadian judges off the bench and using the full force of the state against those in Quebec who continue to obey Ottawa. That means police. That means army. Separatist Daniel Latouche is already on record saying, "Independence is not worth one human life." Stéphane Dion has already invited Lucien Bouchard to renounce the use of force. Like Claude Charron, Bouchard has yet to pronounce himself on the subject.

In July '97, as part of its campaign to assure instant French recognition of a UDI, the government of Quebec invited several French dignitaries to attend provincial ceremonies honouring the unveiling of a statue to General de Gaulle. The dignitaries, including a French presidential emissary, made several incendiary remarks which most governments of sovereign nations would find intolerable.

Bar Entry to French Meddlers

by Keith Henderson:
reprinted from **The Financial Post**
July 29, 1997

Pierre Messmer is a former Prime Minister of France, Phillippe Séguin President Jacques Chirac's personal emissary, Dominique Boché French Consul General. Surrounded by *tricolores* and *fleurs-de-lys,* (no maple leaves, thank you), all three were guests of honour at last week's separatist festival to unveil a statue commemorating the 30th anniversary of de Gaulle's most famous anti-Canadian remark, "Vive le Québec Libre." Never say the French government didn't approve — hardly surprising, since Chirac went on US TV during the '95 referendum campaign and announced that the French would recognize a separatist UDI. Canada didn't protest then, and given the Chrétien-Dion penchant for being sweet to the French, Canada won't protest now. More's the pity.

Not that Séguin and Messmer didn't give us plenty to get angry about. Put aside our own tax dollars spent honouring a foreign general who devoted 10 years of French policy deliberately trying to destroy Canada. Consider what our gracious guests said. Waxing poetic about "the collective liberty of nations who have the right to master their destiny" (French code for unilateral secession), Séguin then quoted a little Nietzsche: "The higher one flies, the smaller one seems to those who cannot fly." In other words, separatists fly. Loyal earthbound Canadians don't fly and so see nothing. The tragic irony behind Séguin's insulting twaddle is that some of the hundreds of veterans gathered in Quebec City to protest this separatist outrage did fly. Over France, risking their lives so people like de Gaulle, Séguin and Messmer could repay their sacrifices by cocking a snoot at them and imperilling the unity of their country. But then who says French presidential emissaries have to keep their feet on the ground?

Messmer went one better. Constitutions? The rule of law? "Paper barriers blown to the wind," he declared. What counts is *"la volonté populaire."* The separatist brainstrust beamed. Their frightening revolutionary stance, "Call a referendum; trash the constitution," the tactic dictators like Napoleon and Hitler repeatedly used to put the patina of legitimacy on their *coups d'états,* had just received more high level French endorsement. To those still on the ground, the consequences of this arrogant anarcho-democrat disease, continental Europe's worst export product, became quickly apparent. Zealous Quebec City police roughed up a poor 65 year-old woman guilty of carrying a Canadian flag to the statue site. The next day separatist goons smashed in the face of an anglo demonstrator at a re-enactment of the de Gaulle's speech on the City Hall steps while some of Montreal's finest looked benignly on in full view of the television cameras. But then, why not? What counts is not the law. It's *"la volonté populaire."*

Where was Ottawa? Stéphane Dion made a few plaintive rejoinders about how our French friends were practising an "uncomfortable" double standard, since the French had declared their own country indivisible and outlawed secession. But the prevailing attitude of federal officials was one of relief. "Look how few really important French dignitaries came," they crowed, as though a personal emissary from the President of France wasn't enough. Dion assured everybody there would be no formal Canadian protest.

Perhaps this is what Lucien Bouchard meant when he said "Canada is not a real country." Real countries don't tolerate what the French have just done. Real countries bar entry to high level officials who come on missions of destruction. Suffering as we do from terminal nice-guy syndrome, Canadians have a hard time with these bitter truths and need to practise a regular régime of 'reverse this' in order to understand how real countries react.

Imagine former Prime Minister Pierre Trudeau has just been invited to Corsica to take part in a Corsican separatist ceremony. Lloyd Axworthy, personal emissary of Jean Chrétien, is going along. The Canadian ambassador to France intends to be there too. Canada's spent 30 years aiding and abetting Corsican separatism, and Jean Chrétien has already been on *Larry King Live* stating that Canada would be the first to recognize the new revolutionary Corsican state. Take 10 seconds. Ask yourself if the French would let this band of Canadian incendiaries into their country. Now ask yourself why we let Phillippe Séguin, Pierre Messmer, and Dominique Boché into ours.

*T*he third major repercussion from the Moot Court meeting was the embryonic discussion, once again long overdue, of whether Canada ought to be indivisible, like most mature G7 democracies, like America or France itself, which hypocritically aids and abets separatism in Canada while outlawing it at home. Were Canada to legalize the procedures of its own dismemberment, it would become one of the few countries in the world to do so, an unenviable anomaly, and yet one the 'right thinking' set that runs the country has never seriously examined. The paradox of Quebec nationalists insisting on the indivisibility of the province's territory — protected by a constitution they won't accept — while negotiating the divisibility of Canada, cannot be lost on Canadians. If Quebec's territory is "sacred and inviolable," to quote Daniel Johnson, why isn't Canada's? The spectacle of Stéphane Dion and other federal leaders never attacking separatism at its root, merely trying to provide it with a legal framework for its noxious effects, can only lead to cynicism and dismay. Canadians have been given countless opportunities, from Meech to Charlottetown to the Calgary Declaration, to turn their country into a pretzel to satisfy nationalists in Quebec, but have never been given the opportunity to decide whether or not their country should be indivisible. BC premier Glen Clark put it well:

> We've got the Quebec premier, the separatist premier, saying that Quebec is not divisible in the event of a referendum. In other words they can't divide Quebec up. Well, I guess the obvious answer is, ... if Quebec is not divisible, then it's about time we said that Canada isn't divisible....

Equality's Brand of Federalism

Gazette *Editorial:*
November 13, 1996

The Equality Party raised many valid points at its annual convention on the weekend. It is right to be concerned about such things as Quebec's referendum law, in particular the weak safeguards against ballot-counting abuse and the law's restrictions on freedom of speech. There is no doubt the law should be improved. Equality members are also right in their opposition to the *Parti Québécois* government's plan to unilaterally declare the independence of Quebec in the event of a YES vote. The PQ's plan is an irresponsible recipe for political and economic chaos and disaster.

But on other issues, Equality is way off base. For starters is party president Keith Henderson's ridiculous claim that his party is the only true Quebec federalist party. It is not because it supports the constitutional *status quo* when it comes to Quebec's concerns that its federalist credentials are more worthy than those of other federalists. It is certainly not by insulting federalists — "the snobbish members of the Quebec establishment" — that Mr. Henderson will advance his cause.

Equally unimpressive was the Equality's motion proposing a national referendum on the "indivisibility of Canada." The party wants a constitutional amendment declaring that Canada is "one and indivisible" just as the French constitution declares that France as now constituted is indivisible. Leaving aside the possibility that such a national referendum might not pass, the Equality idea is a nonstarter. It would be naive to think that such a move could convince Quebecers to vote NO (indeed it risks having the reverse effect) or could keep Quebecers in Canada against their will. Like Equality members, most Canadians, including most Quebecers, do not want Quebec to separate from Canada. But at the same time, most would agree that if a decisive majority of Quebecers wanted to create a separate state, then there should be a way for them to do it.

The difficulty is agreeing on the groundrules, both political and legal. The Bouchard government insists it can set the rules by itself and impose them on the rest of Canada and ignore the rule of law if it so pleases. That position is untenable by any standard. The groundrules and the terms on which Quebec and the rest of Canada would part company should be a matter for both sides to decide. (For example, it is reasonable to insist that the question be clear and that — unlike last year's referendum question — it ask voters if they want to separate from Canada and form an independent country. It is also reasonable to believe that negotiations could take longer than the year, maximum, that the PQ has allowed.) Each side would have rights and responsibilities in such a process. In a politically charged atmosphere, such as the one that could follow a YES vote, it would make sense to ensure that, in addition to respect for the democratic process, there exists a common commitment to the rule of law.

If a decisive majority of Quebecers, in full understanding, were to vote in favour of independence, that would be a political reality the rest of the country could not ignore. That does not mean that Quebec could simply walk out of confederation on its own terms. Negotiations on such things as borders, citizenship, trade relations and the division of assets would have to take place. And, in order for separation to occur legally, the constitution would have to be amended. A unilateral declaration of independence would be a violation of democratic principles and could in no way be justified as long as legal avenues had not been exhausted.

While it is essential to clarify the legal and political issues and clear up confusion about what is at stake, it is equally important for federalists to address the concerns of Quebecers that fuel the separatist movement. They should not overlook Quebec's legitimate concerns and the need to further acknowledge its important role in promoting and safeguarding the country's French character. These efforts stand a better chance than declaring Canada "indivisible" of convincing Quebecers to vote resoundingly for Canada in the event of another referendum. Polls consistently show that a majority of Quebecers would rather stay in Canada, preferably in a renewed federal system, than be part of an independent Quebec state. A party that claims to be federalist shouldn't forget that.

Is Canada Divisible?

by Keith Henderson:
reprinted from the Gazette
November 17, 1996

L ast week, in a piece called 'Equality's brand of Federalism,' the *Gazette* took issue with the party's "ridiculous" claim to be Quebec's only true federalist party. "It is not because it supports the constitutional status quo when it comes to Quebec's concerns that its federalist credentials are more worthy of those of other federalists," the *Gazette* wrote. Yet the editorial refused to deal with why Equality supporters might feel they were the only true federalist alternative in the province.

One reason might be because Equality voted on November 10th to support the federal government's referral of the question of a Quebec UDI to the Supreme Court. Equality supports Ottawa here; Daniel Johnson's Liberals don't. Another reason might be because Equality promised on November 10th never to hold a referendum on Quebec independence and never to propose a Unilateral Declaration of Independence on the floor of the Assembly. Daniel Johnson's Liberals don't agree with either position. "Never say never," Daniel Johnson declared only last month, an attitude which prompted the *Gazette,* in a piece called 'Mr. Johnson's Federalism,' to suggest that Quebec Liberals had "left other federalists scratching their heads." Indeed.

To its credit, the *Gazette* went even further, lamenting the fact that the choice between Lucien Bouchard and Daniel Johnson had become "in effect, Sovereignty or Sovereignty Lite.... It would be nice," the editors concluded, "if [Mr. Johnson] would lose the Bourassian ambiguity in favour of straightforward — and visible — federalism." Mind not too straightforward, now, like that pesky Equality Party. The *Gazette's* tolerance for clarity being perilously low, we can conclude that in the Goldilocks political world of Quebec, no one's federalism is just right.

To be fair, it's Equality's support of a national referendum on the indivisibility of Canada that set the alarm bells running at the *Gazette's* editorial board. "Way off base," was the conclusion, not to mention "naive." But is it? First of all, most mature democracies, having experienced more that just threats of secession, have long ago concluded that making their countries divisible is an eminently bad idea. The French aren't divisible. The Americans and Australians aren't. Just two months ago the Italian government said the idea of national divisibility was a disaster. Everywhere else indivisibility is the norm. Are we Canadians so above other mere mortal nations that we can afford to think otherwise, worse, call those who think the way the rest of our G7 partners do "ridiculous" and "naive?"

The reason why most democracies reject divisibility as an alternative is because no one can agree on how borders are to be set in the event of secession. If one segment of a country wants to hive off, others inside that segment will too. Abraham Lincoln knew this. "Where does the process end?" he asked more than a century ago, West Virginia being still there to prove the justice of his concern. Ethnolinguistic fault lines compound the problem in Quebec, as Canada's only true partitionists, *Péquistes,* are beginning to discover. The first choice we face, as a nation, then, is the to-be-or-not-to-be choice of partition.

'If Canada is divisible, then so is Quebec.' That mantra, federalists should note, is conditional. Is Canada divisible? Should it be? Shouldn't Canadians be asked the question before Stéphane Dion and other unity mavens fly about the country prejudging the answer? If Quebecers knew, in a straightforward and unambiguous way, directly from their federal government, that the partitioning of Canada would lead inevitably to the partitioning of Quebec, would they not perhaps be in favour of indivisibility too? Would the true costs of the secessionist dream not for once be known, in the one context they should be known in — a national context? And if Canadians rejected the indivisibility of their country, as they may, would the federal government not be able to claim, as it cannot now do, that it had a mandate to prepare for the legal break-up of the country?

Can Canada be divided? Can Canadians be deprived of their birthright, the wholeness of their national and provincial territories? The question is timely, relevant, and inescapable. Naive is not to ask it.